HOPE & LIES

101 REASONS TO DEFEAT OBAMA

BY MADDEN

ISBN 978-1-105-31035-5

<u>Foreword</u>

On Tuesday, November 6, 2012, millions of Americans will head to the ballot box to decide the future of this great nation.

Will we elect a leader that is in favor of growing government, increasing the national debt and restricting individual freedom or will we choose a leader that promotes individual freedom, smaller government and less spending? Will we elect someone that will circumvent the U.S. Constitution or someone that will return our nation back to a constitutionally limited government?

CHAPTER 1

The Obamacare Debacle

*Government big enough to supply everything you
need is big enough to take everything you have ...
The course of history shows that as a
government grows, liberty decreases.*

- Thomas Jefferson

1. Obama's "Flagship" accomplishment was built on a mountain of lies

The government takeover of healthcare was rammed through
Congress on a series of lies, distortions and dirty tactics. This
multi-trillion dollar bill that took over one-fifth of the U.S.
economy was forced through Congress before anyone could read
it. This is single-handedly the most important reason to deny
Obama a second term. He cannot be given four more years to
destroy the American dream and implement his radical
transformation of America.

2. Obama lied about Obamacare not raising premiums

Obama guaranteed his plan would lower healthcare premiums by $2,500 a year for the average family. We now know from an analysis by the non-partisan Congressional Budget Office that his European approach to medicine will actually cause the cost of individual insurance to rise by $2,100 per year. That is a huge difference ($4,600) and amounts to a major tax on all hardworking Americans.[i]

3. Obamacare explodes the deficit and creates 159 new Government bureaucracies

From the very beginning until the bitter end of the Obamacare fight, Obama constantly promised that his government takeover of healthcare would reduce the deficit. In fact nothing could be farther from the truth. Significantly growing inefficient government and taking over one-fifth a nation's economy is an economic boondoggle. If left in place, Obamacare will be a deterrent to every future entrepreneurial idea, business model and will destroy the pursuit of individual freedom.

Once fully implemented, Obamacare will drown our economy in massive debt.

According the Congressional Budget Office, the projected cost for the first 10 years of Obamacare is $2.6 trillion, far higher than Obama and Democrat leaders promised. An additional $200 billion in spending will be needed for the Medicare "doctor fix" and an additional $115 billion will be needed just to execute the law.[ii]

4. Obama lied about his Mother being denied health insurance

Candidate Obama and then President Obama repeatedly claimed that his mother died of cancer after being denied health insurance coverage for a preexisting condition. Like so many things Obama reads from his teleprompter this too was a disgusting lie.

Obama made this claim on the campaign trail, during the presidential debates and when pitching Obamacare to the American public. [iii]

Janney Scott a *New York Times* reporter wrote a book, "A Singular Woman: The Untold Story of Barack Obama's Mother," in which she exposes Obama's false claims about his mother's insurance.

As reported by the *Times*, Scott's book quotes "from correspondence from the president's mother to assert that the 1995 dispute concerned a Cigna disability insurance policy and that her actual health insurer had apparently reimbursed most of her medical expenses without argument."[iv]

5. Obama lied about being able to keep your doctor

As Obama was pushing Obamacare onto the American public he repeatedly pledged that everyone would be able to keep their doctor under his healthcare plan. This was just another fib to help pass his radical agenda.

A February 2011 survey of 1,329 U.S. private sector employers by McKinsey & Company,
found that more than 30% of companies will dump healthcare coverage for their employees due to rising costs associated with Obamacare. [v]

As the survey results reported, 30 percent of respondents who said their companies offered employer sponsored health insurance said they would "definitely" or "probably" drop coverage in the years following 2014, the year the Affordable Care Act takes full effect. (Nine percent said "definitely," and 21 percent said "probably.") - Employer Survey on US Healthcare Reform

Despite Obama's claims a third of employers are already planning to jettison their healthcare plans and force their employees to enroll through the state health care exchanges.

6. Obama is forcing Obamacare on us but not on his friends

Remember when Big Labor teamed up with the Obama Administration and started promoting his government takeover of healthcare? If Obamacare is so great why are all these unions requesting and being granted waivers from complying with Obama's new law?

The Hill newspaper reports that 106 new waivers were granted in July 2011 alone, bringing the total to more than 1,500 unions and businesses that have been granted exemptions from Obamacare.

A very high percentage of these waivers have been granted to unions even though unions represent barely 12% of the American workforce.

Odder still is the secrecy in which these wavers are granted. Groups such as Judicial Watch have requested to see the criteria the administration is using to grant these waivers but the Administration has not yet supplied an answer.

Apparently Obamacare is good enough to force on everyone except Obama's friends and his army of campaign volunteers. Perhaps Teamster Boss Jimmy Hoffa words make it clear why they should receive a pass on the biggest government intrusion in our history. When introducing Obama at a union rally earlier this year Hoffa said: "President Obama, this is your army... let's take these sons of bitches out and give America back to America where we belong."

7. Obama lied to Congress regarding Obamacare and illegal immigrants - Congressman Joe Wilson told him so

During a 2009 televised presidential address to a joint session of Congress, President Obama said that illegal immigrants would not benefit under his healthcare plan: "The reforms I am proposing would not apply to those that are here illegally."

Congressman Joe Wilson (R-SC) who was attending the primetime address could not believe what he was hearing and blurted out "You lie!" for the President, the Congress and the entire television watching world to hear. Joe Wilson caught a wrath of heat for his breech of decorum but his taunt was later proven to be true. Obama was indeed lying directly to Congress and to the American public.

In an August 2011 interview on the Fox News Channel, almost two years after the incident, Congressman Wilson set the record straight by reporting that recent government grants totaling $28 million for community healthcare centers nationwide would benefit illegal immigrants.

Wilson went further to say that $8.5 million of the $28.8 million in question was specifically set aside to assist seasonal and migrant farm workers. Wilson also said that the clinics receiving the funds were instructed to not to ask about immigration status.

He told the Fox, "It is clearly providing money that should be going to American citizens not to illegal immigrants…. The president specifically promised the American people that Obamacare would not cover those who are here illegally."[vi]

CHAPTER 2

Crony Capitalism and Corruption

A government that robs Peter to pay Paul can always count on the support of Paul.
- George Bernard Shaw

8. Obama is responsible for taxpayer dollars flowing to Solyndra

Solyndra, the failed green energy company, has become synonymous with everything that is wrong with Washington-corruption, crony capitalism and government waste.

Solyndra, an adorned pet of the Obama Administration was given a sweetheart, government loan (aka taxpayer money) worth $500 million.

This half billion dollar earmark was approved by political appointees amid numerous red flags being raised about the company's viability.

On March 20, 2009, the Department of Energy approved the $535 million loan guarantee. On August 31, 2011 Solyndra announced it was filing for Chapter 11 bankruptcy.

Congressman Darryl Issa (R-CA), Chairman of the House Oversight and Government Reform Committee has launched an investigation into the handling of the Solyndra loan debacle and is planning a series of congressional hearings.

Reports continue to surface that Department of Energy staff as well as staff at the White House saw this coming and warned that Solyndra was headed for bankruptcy.

Fox News reported that several of the president Obama's largest campaign supporters have close ties to Solyndra. George Kaiser, a major investor in Solyndra and a large contributor to Obama coincidentally visited the White House 17 times during the loan approval process.[vii][viii]

Steve Spinner a high level Obama appointee at the Department of Energy raised close to $500,000 for the Obama campaign. Spinner used his position to push for the loan and his wife worked for a firm that was representing Solyndra.[ix]

9. Obama will not let justice get in the way of his election army

One of the most memorable images on the day Barack Obama was elected president was that of a couple of thugs affiliated with the New Black Panthers stationed outside a polling place in Philadelphia waving their nightsticks and scaring voters and poll watchers.

After video of this activity made it to the national news the Justice Department, still under the watch of President George W.

Bush, decided to bring a voter-intimidation case against these men and the New Black Panther Party.

J. Christian Adams and attorney at the Department of Justice was working on the case but before a final judgment could be entered new appointees from the Obama Administration ordered that the charges be dropped.

Adams who resigned from his post shortly after this decision describes what should have been a simple case and an important case for all American voters in a *Newsmax* column.

> *The New Black Panther case was the simplest and most obvious violation of federal law I saw in my Justice Department career. Because of the corrupt nature of the dismissal, statements falsely characterizing the case and, most of all, indefensible orders for the career attorneys not to comply with lawful subpoenas investigating the dismissal, this month I resigned my position as a Department of Justice (DOJ) attorney.*

> *The federal voter-intimidation statutes we used against the New Black Panthers were enacted because America never realized genuine racial equality in elections. Threats of violence characterized elections from the end of the Civil War until the passage of the Voting Rights Act in 1965.*

> *Before the Voting Rights Act, blacks seeking the right to vote, and those aiding them, were victims of violence and intimidation. But unlike the Southern legal system, Southern violence did not discriminate. Black voters were slain, as were the white champions of their cause. Some of the bodies were tossed into bogs and in one case in Philadelphia, Miss., they were buried together in an earthen dam.*

Based on my firsthand experiences, I believe the dismissal of the Black Panther case was motivated by a lawless hostility toward equal enforcement of the law. Others still within the department share my assessment. The department abetted wrongdoers and abandoned law-abiding citizens victimized by the New Black Panthers.

The dismissal raises serious questions about the department's enforcement neutrality in upcoming midterm elections and the subsequent 2012 presidential election.

10. Donors supporting Obama's green agenda get the Taxpayer's green

During a Fox News Sunday interview regarding the Solyndra bankruptcy scandal, Chairman Issa said "We're finding it's not just Solyndra. It's a pattern of these sorts of investments." Weeks later Issa was proven right as another one of the Obama's "pet" green energy companies running off of taxpayer funded loans filed for bankruptcy. This time it was Beacon Power Corp., a green energy storage company.

Beacon filed for bankruptcy just a year after receiving a $43 million loan guarantee from the Department of Energy. The *Daily Caller* first reported that Beacon Power has political fundraising ties to Democrats and Obama but not quite at the exorbitant level of the Solyndra tied donors.

According to the Center for Responsive Politics, Beacon Power president and CEO William "Bill" Capp donated $500 to Obama's presidential campaign. He also donated to Democratic Massachusetts Rep. Niki Tsongas, and to the failed Massachusetts Senate campaign of Democrat Martha Coakley, whom Republican Scott Brown defeated in a special election for the late Sen. Ted Kennedy's open Senate seat.

*Beacon government relations director Matthew E.
Polimeno donated $750 to Rep. Tsongas and $250 to
Coakley. Beacon Power CFO James M. Spiezio also
donated $250 to Coakley.*

*Through their companies, these donors were rewarded
with $17,200 of Energy Department funds for every dollar
they donated to Democrats.[x]*

11. Obama Protecting Friends before Country

On the heels of the Solyndra half billion dollar loan outrage the
Obama Administration was hit with another pay-to-play scandal
and this time it impacted more than just the taxpayers' wallets.
The very safety of our men and women in uniform was
compromised.

In question was the accelerated approval the FCC gave
LightSquared, a wireless broadband company, to get a waiver
allowing the company to use wireless spectrum to build a
wireless 4G network. This approval was quickly granted despite
numerous complaints from the Global Positioning Satellite (GPS)
community that the LightSquared technology has been shown to
overpower and interrupt the weaker GPS signals. These
complaints and concerns have come from military, government
and civilian aviation experts.

The White House worked to downplay these concerns as they
might prevent the approval of the company's project. The White
House even went as far as to pressure high ranking Pentagon
officials to alter their Congressional testimony on the issue.

Air Force General William Shelton and Anthony Russo, Director
of the National Coordination Office for Space-Based Positioning,
Navigation and Timing, both came forward exposing how the

White House pressured each of them to change their testimony and downplay the threat of LightSquared's technology to military communications and navigation.

Why would the Obama Administration be so interested in promoting a project that could harm our military? Could it be to help a donor?? Read this excerpt from Michelle Malkin's column in the *New York Post*. It will leave no doubt about the Administration's motives and further hammers home the need to make Obama a one term president.

So what's greasing LightSquared's skids? Hint: It used to be known as "Skyterra." In 2005, Barack Obama put $50,000 into the speculative firm. The New York Times noted that Skyterra's chief backers at the time included four Obama "friends and donors who had raised more than $150,000 for his political committees."

One pal who urged him to buy stock in Skyterra was George Haywood, a major Skyterra investor, who with his wife chipped in nearly $50,000 to Obama's campaigns and political action committee.

Coincidentally, Obama bought his Skyterra stock the same day the FCC "ruled in favor of the company's effort to create a nationwide wireless network by combining satellites and land-based communications systems." The Times reported that, just after that morning ruling, "Tejas Securities, a regional brokerage in Texas that handled investment banking for Skyterra, issued a research report speculating that Skyterra stock could triple in value."

Tejas and its chairman, John J. Gorman, were also major Obama backers -- flying him in a private plane for rallies and pitching in more than $150,000 for his campaign coffers since 2004. Obama sold his stock at a loss in November 2005, but his relationship with the firm was cemented.

In 2009, billionaire Philip Falcone -- whose hedge-fund firm, Harbinger Capital Partners, is reportedly being *probed by the Securities and Exchange Commission for market-manipulation abuses -- acquired Skyterra. Falcone, his wife and LightSquared CEO Sanjiv Ahuja have contributed nearly $100,000 between them to the Democratic Party during critical White House meeting periods and negotiations over LightSquared's regulatory fate.*

Oh, and there's $6 billion earmarked for a "public-safety broadband corporation" buried in the Obama jobs proposal, just as LightSquared pushes into that market, too.

It's all just one strange quirk of timing, Team Obama shrugs. But there are no coincidences in Chicago on the Potomac, just an endless avalanche of quids, quos and taxpayer woes.[xi]

12. Obama rewards his friends with our money.

Los Angeles Times reporter David Willman broke the news that a $433 million dollar government contract was granted to Siga Technologies, Inc. for the purchase of a smallpox anti-viral drug. The problem is that many in the science and defense world don't think the vaccine is necessary and question if it would even work. There are also some very odd circumstances regarding the way in which this contract was granted.

Willman reported: *"Senior officials have taken unusual steps to secure the contract for New York-based Siga Technologies Inc., whose controlling shareholder is billionaire Ronald O. Perelman, one of the world's richest men and a longtime Democratic Party donor."[xii]*

Forbes in a subsequent article revealed more disturbing facts surrounding this contract.

"The Department of Health and Human Services, having determined that the drug was a needed addition to our bio-terrorism arsenal, appears to have set out to do everything possible -and more- to insure that Siga Technologies won the contract. This included blocking other firms from so much as bidding for the opportunity.

Initially, the contract was put out to bid for small businesses- companies with less than 500 employees. Quickly, the deal was awarded to Siga Technologies. However, Chimerix Inc., a North Carolina based company that also pursued the contract, complained that Siga should have been disqualified for having too many employees - a charge that turned out to be correct.

At that point, HHS could have awarded the contract to Chimerix, a firm that has already done business with the government on smallpox related drugs, or pursued other realistic and reasonable options. HHS could have opened the bidding to larger companies or taken other measures that made sense to expand the competition to find the best company for the job."[xiii]

13. Obama White House tries to bribe senate candidate to drop out of the race

The White House was involved in two electioneering scandals during the 2010 election cycle both times involving Democrat Primary candidates for the U.S. Senate. The first was in the state of Pennsylvania where Congressman Joe Sestak was running for the Democrat nomination against one time liberal Republican and now liberal Democrat Arlen Specter.

Joe Sestak alleged on multiple occasions that the White House approached him and offered him a job if he would drop out of the race. *Politico* reported: Sestak acknowledged in an interview in

February that he was offered a position by an unnamed White House official - a potential violation of federal law.[xiv]

After the Primary, Sestak confirmed the incident again in an interview with NBC reporter David Gregory.[xv]

Sestak defeated Specter in the Democrat primary but would eventually lose the general election to now sitting U.S. Senator Pat Toomey.

14. Electioneering Again

The next scandal on our list is the second scandal involving the Obama White House in U.S. Senate primary electioneering. This one took place in Colorado in a Democrat Primary race that pitted Andrew Romanoff vs. incumbent Senator Michael Bennet. Obama strongly supported Bennet but former president Bill Clinton had come out in support of Romanoff creating an interesting nuance in this race by pitting Obama vs. Clinton by default.

The scandal came about when, like the Joe Sestak scandal in Pennsylvania, the Obama Administration allegedly offered Romanoff an administration job if he would drop out of the race.

On September 27, 2009, *The Denver Post* ran an article stating:

> *Not long after news leaked last month that Andrew Romanoff was determined to make a Democratic primary run against Sen. Michael Bennet, Romanoff received an unexpected communication from one of the most powerful men in Washington.*
>
> *Jim Messina, President Barack Obama's deputy chief of staff and a storied fixer in the White House political shop, suggested a place for Romanoff might be found in the*

administration and offered specific suggestions, according to several sources who described the communication to The Denver Post.

Romanoff turned down the overture, which included mention of a job at USAID, the foreign aid agency, sources said.... "[xvi]

The Obama Administration denied the allegations. Michael Bennet won the nomination and eventually the general election. He is currently representing Colorado in the U.S. Senate.

15. Obama's DOJ suppressing military votes

The men and women in our military put their lives on the line and travel the globe far away from their families and love ones to protect our freedom. The very least our government can do is ensure they have the ability to partake in every election by voting.

Every election we hear about military votes that will not be counted because the absentee ballots were mailed to the servicemen and women too late for them to be returned it in time. Congress tried to correct this by passing the Military and Overseas Voter Empowerment Act in 2009 which requires states to mail their absentee ballots to overseas military and government official at least 45 days before Election Day. This new law only works if the federal government through the Department of Justice enforces it.

The Military Voter Protection Project, a non-profit group, released a study of the law's impact after the 2010 mid-term elections. They concluded while the law did make some good strides but *"questions must be asked and answered regarding DOJ's enforcement of military voting rights in 2010. Military voters should not suffer through another election where DOJ fails to act in a timely manner or fails to fully protect military voters when there has been a clear and egregious violation of federal law."[xvii]*

The study found that "*local election officials in 14 states and the District of Columbia failed to comply with the 45-day standard for mailing absentee ballots. These failures impacted more than 65,000 military and overseas voters....Unfortunately, one state in particular, New York, rejected nearly one-third of all absentee ballots cast and returned by military voters.*"

Why would Obama's Department of Justice fail to enforce this law? Could it be that active military and reservist vote for Republican candidates by a 3 to 1 margin over Democrat candidates?[xviii]

16. Obama's corrupt community of organizers

By now everyone is very familiar with the excessive corruption running amok inside the federally funded "community organizing" group ACORN that was exposed by investigative journalists and filmmakers James O'Keefe and Hanna Giles.

Together they exposed that ACORN was using taxpayer funds to promote and facilitate illegal businesses including illegal immigration and prostitution. After their undercover videos hit the airwaves America was outraged and Congress acted to cut their funding. Despite their efforts many of the ACORN affiliates changed their names and are still working with federal funds.

Perhaps the most important issue brought to light by putting ACORN on center stage was the level of voter fraud being committed by the Acorn organization and just how closely Barack and Michelle Obama were tied to this corrupt group.

Barack Obama got his start in political strategy by working with ACORN as a "community organizer" and a legal representative.

Newsmax exposed the fact that Michelle Obama's "old law firm is representing ACORN's board in an internal embezzlement case that legal experts say could result in criminal charges."

Despite claims from the Obama campaign that they were not in any way affiliated with ACORN during the 2008 Presidential election when the corrupt group was involved in numerous voter registration and voter fraud controversies the records at the Federal Election Commission told a different story.

As reported by *Newsmax*, "[F]ederal election records showed that the Obama campaign paid ACORN subsidiary Citizens Services Inc. $832,598 for get-out-the-vote activities, of which $80,000 went directly to ACORN. CSI and some 290 other ACORN subsidiaries operate out of the same building on Elysian Fields Avenue in New Orleans that serves as ACORN's national headquarters."

CHAPTER 3

Obama's army of Czars

*I don't care who does the electing just so long as
I do the nominating.*
- William "Boss" Tweed

17. If Obama can't get a radical confirmed he will just create a czar

Barack Obama has skirted the Constitution and the Senate confirmation process by appointing "czars" to handle his day to day policy initiatives. While every administration has created a few positions similar to Obama's czars, none have ever appointed so many or created such powerful positions that were not vetted by the U.S. Senate. It is easy to understand Obama's stealthy strategy once one digs into the extremely radical backgrounds of these czars. Obama needs to avoid the confirmation process because they could never be confirmed by the Senate.

Obama's czars are far from mainstream. Many are aligned with communists and socialists. They have fought to eliminate conservative talk radio, actively promoted homosexuality in school, applauded Dictator Hugo Chavez and led the charge to give animals the right to sue in court.

In September 2009, six Republican senators wrote in a letter to the White House stating "The creation of 'czars,' particularly within the Executive Office of the President, circumvents the constitutionally established process of 'advise and consent,' [and] greatly diminishes the ability of Congress to conduct oversight and hold officials accountable. - signed by Sens. Susan Collins (R-ME), Lamar Alexander (R-TN.), Kit Bond (R-MO.), Mike Crapo (R-ID), Pat Roberts (R-KS.) and Bob Bennett (R-UT).

At last count 40 czars have been identified. A few positions have not been filled and there have also been some high profile resignations after political pressure arose about their radical pasts. Most of these czars deserve a standalone spot in the 101 list but that would take too much space. Some of the more outrageous picks did however make the list.

Here is the latest list of Obama Czars:
1. Afghanistan Czar – Richard Holbrooke
2. AIDS Czar – Jeffrey Crowley
3. Auto Recovery Czar – Ed Montgomery
4. Bailout Czar – Neel Kashari
5. Border Czar – Alan Bersin
6. California Water Czar – David J. Hayes
7. Car Czar – Ron Bloom
8. Central Region Czar – Dennis Ross
9. Climate Czar – Todd Stern
10. Copyright Czar – Victoria Espinel
11. Cybersecurity Czar – Howard Schmidt
12. Diversity Czar – Mark Loyd
13. Domestic Violence Czar – Lynn Rosenthal
14. Drug Czar – Gil Kerlikowske
15. Economic Czar – Paul Volcker
16. Energy and Environment Czar – Carol Browner

17. Faith-Based Czar – Joshua DuBois
18. Government Performance Czar – Jeffrey Zients
19. Great Lakes Czar – Cameron Davis
20. Green Jobs Czar – Van Jones (Resigned)
21. Guantanamo Closure Czar – Daniel Fried
22. Health Czar – Nancy-Ann DeParle
23. Information Czar – Vivek Kundra
24. Intelligence Czar – Dennis Blair
25. Labor Czar – Andy Stern
26. Mideast Peace Czar – George Mitchell
27. Pay Czar – Kenneth R. Feinberg
28. Regulatory Czar – Cass R. Sunstein
29. Safe Schools Czar – Kevin Jennings
30. Science Czar – John Holdren
31. Stimulus Accountability Czar – Earl Devaney
32. Sudan Czar – J. Scott Gration
33. TARP Czar – Herb Allison
34. Technology Czar – Aneesh Chopra
35. Tobacco Czar – Lawrence Deyton
36. Terrorism Czar – John Brennan
37. Urban Affairs Czar – Adolfo Carrion Jr.
38. Water Czar – Doulas Lute
39. Weapons Czar – Ashton Carter
40. WMD Policy Czar – Gary Samore

This list was compiled from Glenn Beck's website
(www.Glennbeck.com) and from the book *Shadow Government:
What Obama Doesn't Want You to Know about his Czars* by
Scott Wheeler.

18. Obama's "Safe Schools" Czar is far from safe

Obama's choice for "Safe Schools" czar, Kevin Jennings, is
perhaps the most disgusting and ironic choice of all of his czars.

Kevin Jennings was appointed to this position within the U.S. Department of Education, without any public vetting or U.S. Senate confirmation.

He has a long history of promoting homosexuality in schools and distributing pornographic material to students. He has admitted to past drug use and admitted to covering up illegal man-boy sexual activity when he was a teacher in Massachusetts.

Jennings discussed the incident in his book, *One Teacher In 10: Gay and Lesbian Teachers Tell Their Stories*. He wrote "did not report the sexual victimization of a student to the proper authorities."

This is a very serious offense. A similar incident of alleged "not reporting" was enough to bring down a coaching legend, a university president and leave a permanent black eye on the football program at Penn State University in the fall of 2011.

The bigger problem with Jennings is that he doesn't think he did anything wrong.

As recently as September 28, 2009 a *Washington Times* editorial stated that, Jennings had "not admitted that he made a mistake in this case and he now refuses to answer any questions about the scandal." [xix]

19. Obama's radical Science is dangerous to the human race

John Holdren, Obama's Science Czar is a left wing radical with a decades-long resume of peddling the catastrophe-du-jour to advance his big government, anti-capitalist agenda. He is one of the leaders in pushing the "global warming" myth yet in the 1970s he was a leader pitching a new catastrophic "ice age."

John Holdren serves as the director of the White House's Office of Science and Technology Policy, advising the president on scientific affairs, focusing on energy and "global warming." Holdren's ideas about public policy and government control are extreme even for the Obama Administration.

Holdren has endorsed the idea of forced abortions, and compulsory sterilization. He has also promoted the idea of creating a "planetary regime" that would oversee human population levels and have the authority to control all natural resources in an effort to protect the earth. [xx]

Holdren was also a prominent name exposed in the climate "email gate" when the email system from the University of East Anglia's Climate Research Unit, one of the world's leading climate research facilities, was breeched, exposing the largest scientific fraud in history. These emails detail a concerted effort to hide, manipulate, and destroy any scientific data contradicting global warming.

The Canada Free Press reported that Holdren was prominently featured in the thousands of the hacked email. One email contained a 2003 exchange between Holdren and Nick Schulz, the editor-in-chief of Tech Central Station in which Schulz questioned Holdren on whether choosing to ignore the importance of the Medieval Warm Period required "what lawyers call the burden of proof."[xxi] The Medieval Warm Period, from 800 – 1200 A.D., completely undermines the man-made global warming scam because the spike in global temperatures occurred well before the industrial revolution and human production of greenhouse gases.

Holdren responded "[I]n practice, burden of proof is an evolving thing-it evolves as the amount of evidence relevant to a particular proposition grow." [xxii] This response is astounding yet very revealing. The burden of proof does not change in science but political agendas and the sources of government grants do change.

20. A czar too far – Van Jones

Van Jones is probably the most famous or infamous of Obama czars. Jones was picked to serve as the president's "Green Jobs" czar.

Shortly after being appointed to his new position Jones became a lightning rod for the Administration and the poster child of all that is wrong with Obama's growing regime of czars.

Eventually the public outrage escalated to a level that forced Jones to resign from this dubious post but is important to point out the White House never once disavowed any of Jones' past actions, statements, views or associations.

Here are just a few reasons Jones should have never been given a job with any White House and why he made the 101 list.

Jones was closely associated with the communist revolutionary organization STORM and claims he had become a communist. [xxiii]

He claimed that "white polluters and white environmentalists are essentially steering poison into the people of color communities."[xxiv]

He used over-the-top profanity when describing Republican lawmakers at a February 11, 2009, Berkeley, CA conference, a crude display that is always becoming of a White House official. [xxv]

Jones alleged the United States government deliberately allowed the September 11th attacks to occur and even signed a petition affirming this belief.[xxvi]

21. The Regulatory Czar dislikes all things American

Cass Sunstein, Obama's Regulatory Czar is in charge of the powerful Office of Information and Regulatory Affairs (OIRA). Sunstein is a radical anti-gun, anti-hunting, pro-tax, pro-universal healthcare, radical that would like to regulate conservative talk radio and Internet blogs into extinction.

In Sunstein's role he is responsible for overseeing the development and implementation of all government wide standards and regulations. Regulations and taxes are the two heaviest burdens borne by any business and this guy is in control of one of them.

Sunstein is an advocate of using government to "nudge" people into making what he deems are "better decisions." He outlines this need for government power in his book *Nudge: Improving Decisions about Health, Wealth, and Happiness*.

Since Obama took office the regulatory burden due to new rules and regulations has been greater than any other Administration in history. With an extremist like Sunstein at the helm it is no wonder we have a runaway EPA and OSHA.

Cass Sunstein is also a radical animal rights activist. He takes his beliefs so far that has argued for and promoted giving the right to bring legal suit on behalf of animals. Until this guy leaves office all pet owners, hunters and meat lovers should beware!

CHAPTER 4

A picture is worth a thousand votes

*Humility and knowledge in poor clothes excel
pride and ignorance in costly attire.*
- William Penn

22. Obama photo opt scares and outrages millions of New Yorkers

In the role of commander-in-chief, the President should make Americans feel safe not scare the hell out of them.

In one of the most arrogant and naive actions since Obama took the oath of office, the White House scared millions of New Yorkers and brought back horrible memories of September 11, 2001 for a political photo-op.

On April 27, 2009 the White House authorized a photo shoot involving Air Force One and a fighter jet flying at low altitude around the Island of Manhattan. The President was not on board the plane at the time but the indelible images of a low flying jetliner with a fighter jet escort was enough to frighten millions of residents in lower Manhattan.

New York City Mayor Michael Bloomberg said he was "furious" about the low-altitude flyover near Ground Zero and called it "ill-conceived" and a "waste of taxpayers' money."[xxvii]

Numerous buildings in lower Manhattan were evacuated as a result of the scare and an airport official told ABC News. "It scared a couple of million people."[xxviii]

There is no word on how the photo turned out.

23. A photo at any price

On Friday, August 5, 2009 thirty of America's bravest soldiers gave their lives during an operation to capture a Taliban leader in Afghanistan. This tragic helicopter crash would mark the deadliest incident suffered by the United States during the 10 year war in Afghanistan.

A few days later, President Obama attended the military ceremony, called a "dignified transfer," at Dover Air Force Base which serves as the entry point for all remains of U.S. troops killed overseas.

The Associated Press reported that "Pentagon officials had said that because 19 of 30 of the American families of the dead had objected to media coverage of the remains coming off a plane at Dover Air Force Base, no images could be taken. In addition, the Pentagon rejected media requests to take photos that showed officials at the ceremony but did not depict caskets."

Media coverage at the base is only allowed when family members of the fallen soldiers approve it. This policy and this solemn occasion however did not stop the Obama White House from taking advantage of the photo op and trying to score political points.

A White House photographer took and widely distributed a photo of Obama at the ceremony. These brave soldiers certainly deserve to have the Commander-and-Chief greet and salute them on their final journey but they and their families do not deserve to have their wishes ignored and to have this very personal moment turned into a political stunt.

24. Look at me, not him!

Ever the classy statesman and politician looking for the next photo shoot, Obama has made a habit of bad photos. Perhaps none speak louder than the official photo at the "Open Government Partnership" conference at the United Nations on September 20, 2011.

During the official photo while more than two dozen world leaders stood still, Obama felt the need to spice up the photo and bring additional attention to himself by waving to the camera. The problem with his narcissistic move is that his now waving hand fully blocked the face of the president of Mongolia who was standing behind him. The official photo can still be seen on the Getty Images website.

CHAPTER 5

Decorum and Etiquette have been thrown out

Etiquette requires us to admire the human race.
- Mark Twain

25. Obama hosted a vile poet and now we all know it

In May 2011, the White House hosted a poetry reading event in which Michelle Obama invited vile rapper "Common" (Lonnie Rashid Lynn, Jr.).

The inclusion of Lynn at this event was met with harsh criticism from family groups, Republicans and police unions. The White House's choice to include Lynn was beyond reproach considering the type of vitriolic, violence inciting lyrics that are frequently produced by the hip hop singer.

Some of Lynn's more controversial poetry includes threats to shoot police and a call for the "burn[ing]" of President George W. Bush.[xxix]

The New Jersey state police was outraged about Lynn's inclusion because the rapper has a song, "Song for Assata" that honors convicted cop-killer Assata Shakur. Shakur formerly known as Joanne Chesimard, was found guilty for the murder New Jersey State Trooper Werner Foerster in 1973. Shakar successfully escaped prison in 1979 and is reported to be living in asylum in Cuba.[xxx]

26. To bow or not to bow

Miss Manners, the gold standard when it comes to etiquette advice states "One does not bow or curtsy to a foreign monarch because the gesture symbolizes recognition of her power over her subjects."

Perhaps someone should send a copy to President Obama before he succumbs to the presences of perceived leadership during another trip abroad.

When greeting the King of Saudi Arabia during an April 2009 trip, the President opted to go with a full blown bow from the waist, a move he later tried to deny.

His chosen style for greeting appeared especially awkward since none of the other guests including world leaders and spouses chose to bow instead opting for a traditional handshake.

His move was described aptly by Clarice Feldman in an *American Thinker* commentary: "I am quite certain that this is not the protocol, and is most unbecoming a president of the United States."

Obama is apparently a big fan of the bow because he was caught bowing again to greet Japanese Emperor Akihito just seven months later.

27. The strange gift exchange

In a move that brought real class and dignity to the Oval Office and truly elevated the "office of the president" to new heights, President Obama showered British Prime Minister Gordon Brown with gifts when he came for a visit. This exchange of gifts is a formal protocol of diplomacy that far outdates Obama's political career.

The only problem is that Obama's gift choice created an embarrassing diplomatic mess. Gordon Brown presented Obama with a pencil holder carved from the timbers of the anti-slave ship, HMS Resolute, the very same historic timbers from which the President's oval office desk is made.

Obama countered this thoughtful gift with a set of not so historic DVDs. Adding insult to injury, the DVDs that Gordon Brown was now the proud owner of did not work abroad and were unwatchable when he returned to London.

This isn't the only awkward - to say the least - gift exchange with the British. When Obama met with Queen Elizabeth in Buckingham Palace in April 2009 he gave the aging Queen an IPod. Her new high-tech gadget was preloaded with Obama speeches on it among other things.

The Obama's also made a great impression on the faculty and alumni of their daughters' prestigious $33,000 a year school when presenting their gift for the school's annual auction.

When the Clintons sent Chelsea to the same school, they participated in the auction by donating items with a personal touch like dinners, lunches and even babysitting. The Obama's chose to offer signed pictures of themselves.

28. Dissing the British National Anthem

If you have not had the opportunity to see this web gem you owe yourself the pleasure of watching one of the more hilarious yet gut cringing videos on the Internet today. Search the words (Obama toast god save the queen) and watch it on YouTube, just refrain from putting any liquid in your mouth until your done watching the entire video.

As a way of background, Obama was visiting Buckingham Palace and was given the opportunity to toast the Queen. It is formal protocol and just simple etiquette to remain silent anytime the band strikes up *God Save the Queen*, the British National Anthem. This protocol is even more important when inside the walls of Buckingham Palace and especially when standing mere inches from... you guessed it – the Queen.

Instead of taking a cue from the hundreds of other dignitaries in the room at the time who were properly following the silent protocol, Obama chose to use the anthem as background music for his blabbering toast. Meanwhile the Queen refuses to make eye contact with Obama and by the end of the toast appears to have moved through several emotional stages from astonishment to anger to near laughter at the "dumb" American.

29. Running out on the tab to leave Chicago taxpayers with his "party" bill

Obama was roundly criticized for throwing an election celebration that far out did the election victory celebrations of any previous victors. Instead of the normal hotel ballroom/conference room for poll watching and speeches, Obama opted for a much more gaudy and elaborate venue by renting out Grant Park, one of Chicago's largest parks and addressing a crowd of over 240,000.[xxxi]

The Obama campaign and the Democratic National Committee were in no hurry to pay for this election night extravaganza. The *Chicago Sun-Times* ran a story on February 20 more than a hundred days after the election party reporting that the $1.74 million dollar tab run up by the Obama campaign had not been paid.[xxxii]

Chicago at the time was suffering through a $50.5 million budget shortfall and many had criticized the city for even allowing such an event. The *Sun-Times* reported that Mayor Daley noted in October that the city had a "financial crisis" and that "The City of Chicago could not afford $2 million on this because we're gonna be laying off people, cutting back. . . It's a huge cost to the City of Chicago." Mayor Daley (who would eventually become Obama's Chief of Staff) was assured that the "cash-flush" Obama campaign would reimburse the city so he got behind and supported the celebration plan.

On March 22, 2009 the *Huffington Post* reported that the Democrat National Committee finally paid $1.74 million debt to Chicago for the November 4, 2008 party.[xxxiii]

30. Calling the Tea Party racist

Obama has been critical and dismissive of the Tea Party movement from the beginning. Perhaps his inability to recognize the movement as genuine and his inability to refrain from attacking them helped galvanize the movement that lead to the historic mid-term election of 2010.

In May 2010, Obama addressed a private White House dinner in which he stated that race was a key component of the Tea Party movement. Ironic how one year later, Herman Cain, an African American, is leading the Tea Party effort to make Obama a one term president.

Obama's comments and actions can only be overshadowed by his gaffe prone Vice President who was unleashed during the debt ceiling debate to attack the Tea Party. Biden chose to label the Tea Party affiliated members of Congress trying to rein in spending as "terrorists."

It's hard to imagine the cataclysmic uproar that would have ensued if Vice President Cheney had done the same thing to any Democrat constituency during the Bush years.

31. Obama embraces and praise the "Occupy" movement

Obama and his allies relentlessly attacked the Tea Party movement but they have embraced the "Occupy" Wall Street movement. Obama even told a group of Occupy protestors at an event in Manchester, New Hampshire that ""You are the reason I ran for office."[xxxiv]

Giving this anarchist, anti-capitalist movement credit for his presidential run is shocking when compared to the racist, violent and terrorist labels Obama and his surrogates so quickly and so often throw at the Tea Party.

Let us not forget that the "Occupy" movement is endorsed by the American Nazi Party, the Socialist Party USA, the Communist Party USA and other anti-freedom groups[xxxv]. The "Occupy" Wall Street movement has cost cities across America millions. The *Associated Press* reported "*During the first two months of the nationwide Occupy protests, the movement that is demanding more out of the wealthiest Americans cost local taxpayers at least $13 million in police overtime and other municipal services.*"[xxxvi] This was just for the first two months.

The "Occupy" marches and tent cities have led to thousands of arrests, allegations of rape, vandalism, rampant drug use, and even death.

Is this anti-American mob really something we want our President embracing?

32. Sitting thru Hugo Chavez rant

In April 2009, Obama attended the Fifth Summit of the Americas in Trinidad and Tobago with leaders from South American countries. During the summit President Obama accepted a gift from the American hating Venezuelan President/Dictator Hugo Chavez. It's bad enough that the President of the United States would even shake the hand of this vitriolic man nevertheless pose for a photo op with him and accept his gift.

The gift in question was a copy of "Open Veins of Latin America: Five Centuries of the Pillage of a Continent" by Uruguayan author Eduardo Galeano, a book harshly critical of the United States' economic and foreign affairs policies.

After accepting the gift, Obama sat through a series of anti-American speeches from Chavez as well as one from Nicaraguan President Daniel Ortega to which his response after was "I am very grateful that President Ortega didn't blame me for things that happened when I was three months old."[xxxvii]

That's leadership!

33. Charging your guests - Biden collects rent from the Secret Service

The Washington Times has reported that Vice President Biden receives $26,400 dollars a year from the Secret Service in the form of rent. The Secret Service pays Biden with our tax dollars.

The rent comes from fees the Biden's charge the Secret Service for setting up their life protecting and national security service at a cottage on lakefront property the Bidens own in Delaware. The Secret Service is required to be there to protect Biden when he frequently visits this home.

The *Times* reports that the Secret Service approved a purchase order in November 2011 to pay Mr. Biden $26,400 for rent on the building for the next twelve months.

Vice President Biden's personal office told the *Times* that the cottage had been occupied by Mr. Biden's mother, Jean Biden, who died in 2010 at the age of 92.[xxxviii]

CHAPTER 6

Pants on Fire

The truth is incontrovertible. Malice may attack it, ignorance may deride it, but in the end, there it is.-

Sir Winston Churchill

34. Obama lies to scare seniors and veterans for political gain

In the summer of 2011, the Congress was in a heated debate over whether or not to increase the nation's debt ceiling. The debt ceiling places a limit on how much the U.S. can borrow. If Congress had decided to stop raising the debt ceiling years ago we would not be a nation drowning in a debt of more than $15 trillion.

Obama afraid that Congress might for once act responsibly and balance the country's checkbook the same way every American family and business must… he stoops to the lowest possible political tactics. He hits the national airwaves threatening that seniors and veterans would not receive their Social Security and pension checks unless Congress acted immediately.

"I cannot guarantee that those checks go out...if we haven't resolved this issue. Because there may simply not be the money in the coffers to do it...this is not just a matter of Social Security checks. These are veteran's checks, these are folks on disability and their checks. There are about 70 million checks that go out." Obama told CBS News.

This disgraceful political stunt was a blatant lie. Social Security checks and veterans' pension checks were never in jeopardy of not going out.

Terrence Jeffrey with, *CNSNews* analyzed the Daily Treasury Statements published by the U.S. Treasury Department, and reported that " the ongoing flow of federal tax revenue since the Treasury declared that it had hit the debt limit on May 16 has been more than sufficient to cover the combined costs of federal spending on interest payments, Medicare, Medicaid, Social Security, the Veterans Affairs department and federal workers wages and insurance benefits (including wages and insurance benefits for military personnel).[xxxix]

35. The Caterpillar lie

In February 2009, Obama was caught in a lie about the impact his so-called "stimulus" bill he was trying to get Congress to pass would have on the American economy.

At a press conference Obama claimed that Caterpillar CEO, Jim Owens told him that if Congress passes the stimulus plan he will be able to rehire some of the 22,000 employees the company just laid off. Obama repeated this claim at an event in Peoria, Illinois the following day.

There was one big problem. Jim Owens never told that to Obama and the claim of rehiring was simply not true.

Jim Owens spoke to ABC News after the Peoria event and said that the stimulus plan would not stop the layoffs and that additional layoffs would still be expected before the company started rehiring again. When asked if the stimulus would allow the re-hiring those laid off Owens stated, "I think realistically no. The truth is we're going to have more layoffs before we start hiring again."[xl]

36. Obama lied about cutting the deficit in half by end of first term

Early in President Obama's first year in office he pledged that he would cut the deficit in half.[xli] This is perhaps the most outrageous and blatant lie that he has thrown at the American people.

After three years of excessive regulation and government spending it is no surprise that he failed to stimulate the economy and cut the deficit in half. On February 14, 2011 the Office of Management and Budget released the Fiscal Year 2012 Budget where the deficit is expected to be $1.1 trillion more than double Obama's pledge.

37. He lied about covering the healthcare debates on C-SPAN

On the campaign trail Obama promised to make the healthcare debate a transparent process by airing the negotiations on C-SPAN. Breitbart TV compiled a video montage of Obama making the C-SPAN promise eight separate times.

This was apparently just another lie. Instead of airing the controversial negotiations the healthcare bill was crafted in secret behind closed doors.

Brian Lamb the CEO of C-SPAN wrote a letter to Congressional leaders urging them to allow the network to cover the healthcare meetings. The letter stated: "The C-SPAN networks will commit the necessary resources to covering all of the sessions LIVE and in their entirety."[xlii]

This request and the request of the American public for Obama to follow up on his promise to negotiate this bill in the open fell flat. Instead the bill was rushed through before anyone in Congress or anyone in the public had an opportunity to read and comment on the two thousand page bill.

38. Obama said he wouldn't hire lobbyists

Obama pledged that lobbyists "won't find a job in my White House" while campaigning in November of 2008.[xliii] This was a pledge that he used to cast himself as a "new" kind of politician.

Politico analyzed the Obama Administration's hiring and published a story on January 28, 2009 just days after Obama took the oath of office that showed this pledge of no lobbyist was just another one of Obama's campaign lies to the American public.[xliv]

Politico reported that at least a dozen former lobbyists had "found top jobs in his administration"

The list as reported by *Politico*[xlv]:
- Eric Holder, attorney general nominee, was registered to lobby until 2004 on behalf of clients including Global Crossing, a bankrupt telecommunications firm.

- Tom Vilsack, secretary of agriculture nominee, was registered to lobby as recently as last year on behalf of the National Education Association.
- William Lynn, deputy defense secretary nominee, was registered to lobby as recently as last year for defense contractor Raytheon, where he was a top executive.
- William Corr, deputy health and human services secretary nominee, was registered to lobby until last year for the Campaign for Tobacco-Free Kids, a non-profit that pushes to limit tobacco use.
- David Hayes, deputy interior secretary nominee, was registered to lobby until 2006 for clients, including the regional utility San Diego Gas & Electric.
- Mark Patterson, chief of staff to Treasury Secretary Timothy Geithner, was registered to lobby as recently as last year for financial giant Goldman Sachs.
- Ron Klain, chief of staff to Vice President Joe Biden, was registered to lobby until 2005 for clients, including the Coalition for Asbestos Resolution, U.S. Airways, Airborne Express and drug-maker ImClone.
- Mona Sutphen, deputy White House chief of staff, was registered to lobby for clients, including Angliss International in 2003.
- Melody Barnes, domestic policy council director, lobbied in 2003 and 2004 for liberal advocacy groups, including the American Civil Liberties Union, the Leadership Conference on Civil Rights, the American Constitution Society and the Center for Reproductive Rights.
- Cecilia Munoz, White House director of intergovernmental affairs, was a lobbyist as recently as last year for the National Council of La Raza, a Hispanic advocacy group.
- Patrick Gaspard, White House political affairs director, was a lobbyist for the Service Employees International Union.
- Michael Strautmanis, chief of staff to the president's assistant for intergovernmental relations, lobbied for the American Association of Justice from 2001 until 2005.

39. Obama claims we all want higher taxes

During the fight over whether or not to raise the nation's debt ceiling in the summer of 2011, Obama made the outrageous claim that that Americans want higher taxes. Obama claimed that 80 percent of the public supports his demand for tax increases.[xlvi]

On higher taxes he said "The American people are sold…This is not an issue of salesmanship to the American people.[xlvii]"

Human Events called the White House out for such an absurd statement and pointed to a Rasmussen poll taken the same week Obama made the statements showing only 34 percent believe a tax hike should be included in a debt-ceiling agreement. [xlviii]

I think it is safe to say that Obama's near miss of accuracy by 50 percentage points falls outside the margin of error in any modern poll. This was just another lie being thrown at the American public in an attempt to grow government power and redistribute wealth.

40. Obama almost immediately broke his campaign pledge of "No Earmarks."

President Obama took a no-earmark pledge on the presidential campaign trail.[xlix] He broke this promise almost immediately and exposed another campaign lie that he had stopped requesting earmarks while a U.S. Senator.

During a presidential debate on September 26, 2008, candidate Obama stated that he had stopped requesting earmarks as a senator and went further to echo his opponent Senator John

McCain's desire for earmark reform and the elimination of wasteful pork projects.

During this exchange on earmarks Obama said "[A]nd when I'm president, I will go line by line to make sure that we are not spending money unwisely."

Neither of Obama's earmark promises came true. While he claimed he had stopped requesting earmarks in 2008 he is clearly named as one of the cosponsors of a $7.7 million earmark in the fiscal 2009 omnibus spending bill.[l]

Despite calling for earmark reform eliminating pet projects, Obama signed the Omnibus Appropriations Act of 2009, a $410 billion spending bill stuffed with nearly 9,000 earmarks.[li]

In addition to signing the earmark laden Omnibus bill he signed the $787 billion economic stimulus bill which also included plenty of earmarks all within his first several months in the oval office.

41. He lied about no new taxes for middle class and working poor

While on the campaign trail candidate Obama made several tax pledges including this one: *"Under my plan, no family making less than $250,000 will see their taxes increase – not your income taxes, not your payroll taxes, not your capital gains taxes, not any of your taxes."* - Dover, N.H., on September 12, 2008.

This so-called promise lasted less than one month after he took office. On February 4, Obama signed a law to increase the federal excise tax on tobacco by 156%. This increase amounts to a 61 cents per pack of cigarettes. Tobacco taxes place a much higher burden on than the working poor than any other group.

The Americans for Tax Reform have reported that 55% of all smokers fall into the category of "working poor."

Anyone doubting the Obama Administration's desire to raise taxes on the middle class needs to look no further than Obamacare. The individual mandate provision in Obamacare which is currently being challenged in the courts as unconstitutional, forces all Americans to purchase healthcare or pay a hefty fine. The Obama Administration should know that even if you call a tax a fine it is still a tax.

42. The big transparency lie

On the campaign trail candidate Obama made a big deal about "government transparency" and made claims that his White House would be the most transparent administration in history.

One of Obama's first actions as president was to issue a memo pledging "an unprecedented level of openness in government."[lii] This memo and all of his campaign trail pledges on transparency were obviously just for show.

According to the *Wall Street Journal*, "the Obama Administration is not only less transparent than promised but in many ways more opaque than its predecessors." [liii]

Candidate Obama pledged to air the Obamacare negotiations on C-SPAN. This didn't happen.

He pledged to post all bills on the Internet for five days before signing. This didn't happen

Obama said he would make all White House meetings with lobbyists more open. This didn't happen. In fact just the opposite is true.

Kim Strassel with the *Wall Street Journal* cited a study by the Center for Public Integrity showing that "only 1% of 500,000 meetings from the president's first eight months have been released, and thousands of known visitors (including lobbyists) are missing from the lists."

Congressman Cliff Stearns (R-FL), chairman of the House Energy and Commerce Oversight Subcommittee stated during a May 2001 hearing that White House staff has been reported to "go to great lengths to avoid disclosing their meetings with lobbyists…. White House staff apparently purposely schedule meetings at the Caribou Coffee around the corner from the White House so that those meetings won't show up on the White House logs." [liv]

In the irony of all ironies, the *Daily Caller* published a story about a top secret transparency meeting put together by the White House. The purpose of the closed-door secret transparency meeting was to discuss the handling of Freedom of Information requests.[lv]

43. He lied about posting bills on the Internet

While on the campaign trail, Obama pledged to post every bill passed by Congress online for five days before signing the legislation.

"When there's a bill that ends up on my desk as president, you the public will have five days to look online and find out what's in it before I sign it, so that you know what your government's doing."

This lie was made in an effort to give the public the impression that he wanted them to have a fair opportunity to review the often hundred page or even thousand page bills and have an opportunity to comment.

As reported by the *New York Times,* just five months into his presidency it was clear that the White House wasn't going to follow through on that five-day pledge.

Letting the public review bills before signing was never a true desire. We all know now that most Members of Congress never even read the bills they vote on. In Speaker Pelosi's now infamous words "We need to pass the bill so we can find out what's in the bill."

Don't forget about Senator Max Baucus (D-MT), chairman of the Finance Committee and key drafter of Obamacare stating "I don't think you want me to waste my time to read every page of the health care bill."

Apparently no one is supposed to read the legislation coming from Capitol Hill. We are just supposed to comply with the laws they enact.

44. Obama lies about US oil production

On numerous occasions including a May 26, speech in Indianapolis, President Obama stated that the U.S. is producing "more oil than ever."[lvi]   This statement is simply not true.

Obama's oil lie is a blatant attempt to ease the public's anger over his anti-American oil policies that are destroying jobs and increasing energy prices during a recession. Obama's anti-energy crusade can rightly be considered the greatest hindrance to getting our economy going again.

In 1970 we were producing 9.6 million barrels per day. In 2010, the U.S. produced about 5.5 million barrels per day. How is this more oil than ever? Obama makes this outrageous statement on the heels of placing a moratorium on new oil production in the Gulf of Mexico and refusing to approve the Keystone XL pipeline that would bring Canadian crude to U.S. refineries. Canada has the second largest oil reserves in the world and this pipeline would create more than 500,000 American jobs.

45. Obama lied about the auto bailouts

In June 2011, Obama made a special trip to Ohio to lie to the American public about the success of the auto bailout. He later continued his charade by making it the subject of his weekly radio address.

Obama made the claim that "Chrysler has repaid every dime and more of what it owes American taxpayers for their support during my presidency - and it repaid that money six years ahead of schedule. And this week, we reached a deal to sell our remaining stake. That means soon, Chrysler will be 100 percent in private hands."

There is one enormous catch to Obama's claim.

It is a lie of omission. He is only counting the second $8.5 billion loan the government made to Chrysler under his watch and excludes the $4 billion that President George W. Bush loaned during the last days off his term[lvii] (a move Obama fully supported).

The auto bailout was another bad government decision. A decision made by the Washington establishment citing the "too big to fail" mantra.

On November 15, 2011 the *Detroit Daily News* reported that the U.S. Treasury had revised its numbers regarding the auto bailout total cost. The Treasury determined that the impact to the American taxpayer will be a loss of $23.6 billion.

Obama is a full hearted believer that the government has the responsibility of picking winners and losers by implementing wealth re-distributive mechanisms. Even though Obama lies about the auto bailout we all know he must be proud of this redistribution.

CHAPTER 7

Are you kidding me? Come on man!

A politician thinks of the next election - a statesman of the next generation.
- James Freeman Clarke

46. Military decisions and politics don't mix

On June 22, 2011 President Obama announced that 10,000 troops will be withdrawn from Afghanistan by the end of the year and a total of 33,000 troops will be withdrawn by next summer. Obama's announcement went against the requests and advice from Pentagon officials including General David Petraeus. General Petraeus and his top commanders on the ground wanted to limit the initial troop withdrawal to under 4,000 troops and spread the more extensive withdrawal out over a longer period of time.

Mike Brownfield, a military expert at the Heritage Foundation wrote in a June 23 piece, *"The President's decision, though politically expedient, jeopardizes the successes made in Afghanistan over the last 10 months and will signal to allies and enemies alike that the United States is more committed to extricating itself from the fight than it is to ensuring that stability in the region is achieved.* "[lviii]

Senator John McCain criticized the President's decision stating "*I am concerned that the withdrawal plan that President Obama announced tonight poses an unnecessary risk to the hard-won gains that our troops have made thus far in Afghanistan and to the decisive progress that must still be made. This is not the "modest" withdrawal that I and others had hoped for and advocated.* "[lix]

Our troops have been fighting terrorism in Afghanistan for ten years with much success. It is shameful to think that a Commander-in-Chief would jeopardize the long term success of their efforts for a short political gain. This decision should have been based on the recommendations of his military commanders on the ground and not on the advice of his political advisers scrounging for votes.

47. Obama is gutting our national defense

Obama is again playing politics with our military. Obama refused to propose any spending cuts during the heated debt ceiling debate or the subsequent spending fight allocated to the "Super Committee" (a doomed-to-fail group Congress threw together) yet Obama is going to allow a spending trigger he signed into law gut the nation's military by more than half a trillion dollars.

This cut comes on the heels of an earlier 400 billion spending cut.[lx]

Lt. Colonel Oliver North summed it up in an interview with Fox's Martha MacCallum:

We've never before disarmed in the midst of a war. And the problem is this president said he will veto any measure that would reverse it. It's the largest defense cut in military history and it will yield us the smallest military force since before World War II. We are looking at cuts in military and DOD civilian personnel, military construction cuts which will leave unfinished buildings and bases, and of course weapons systems like ships that won't get finished. You can't build and sail three quarters of a ship. You can't build enough F-35 drone strike fighters, do research and development on everything from new anti-aircraft to new air-ground missiles for the new predators and reapers and the next generation of these so- called drone's. And you can't upgrade our M1 tanks or build ground combat vehicles. It goes on and on. And what they have done is basically left us in harm's way.[lxi]

Again our military deserves better.

48. The infamous "Beer Summit"

This is an example of why Obama is rarely allowed off the teleprompter. During a July 2009 press conference Obama chose to answer a question about a local Cambridge, Massachusetts issue which he admittedly knew nothing about. Instead of passing on the question, he answered and opened up a huge can of worms his political advisers wish he hadn't. To fix it he eventually had to open a can a beer in what became a countrywide spectacle.

During the press conference Obama answered a question about a then-recent incident between the Cambridge police and Henry Louis Gates, an Obama acquaintance.

In his response Obama admitted that he should not have answered it - "not having been there and not seeing all the facts…" Unfortunately for the President he could not help himself and answered anyway. He declared "the Cambridge police acted stupidly" – an accusation he admitted literally just seconds before that he has no way of knowing was true.

After Obama responded, this issue erupted into the biggest race issue of the year. Henry Louis Gates, an African American, claimed that the Cambridge police were wrongly race profiling him when responding to a house who's front door had been kicked in. Now the leader of the free world was weighing in.

After this issue wouldn't go away, Obama's only way out was to invite Mr. Gates and Sargent James Crowley, the police officer at the center of the complaint, to the White House to have a beer and discuss race relations.

The White House meeting which will forever be known as the "Beer Summit" took place on took place on July 29, 2009. This was a complete waste of time and more importantly a waste of some good suds.

49. Campaigning is not leading

Barack Obama is known more for his campaigning than his leading. He has even been dubbed by many as the "campaigner-in-chief." Obama's decision to persistently campaign in swing states instead of staying in Washington to lead Capitol Hill negotiations raises valid concerns as to who should be paying for these political trips. Campaign trips are supposed to be paid for by the campaign not the taxpayer but that is not the case for Obama's series of political stump speeches promoting politics not policy.

A November 28, 2011 *Wall Street Journal* article by Jonathon Weisman and Carole Lee pointed out:

"When President Barack Obama jets to Scranton, Pa., Wednesday to promote his jobs package, he'll log his 56th event in a presidential battleground state this year, putting him well ahead of President George W. Bush's record-breaking swing-state travel in 2003.

Mr. Obama's extensive travels this year have opened the president to criticism from Republicans that he is intertwining campaigning and governing at a time when he has called for bipartisanship on intractable national problems. Most of the cost is typically borne by taxpayers."[lxii]

ABC World News reporter Jake Tapper referenced the *Journal's* report stating, "It looks like the President's campaigning on the taxpayers' dime more than any other President has done."[lxiii]

50. Joe Biden - enough said

While the Vice President is great for the late night talk shows his bumbling ways are not good for America.

Joe Biden's gaffes have become so infamous that entire websites have been created just to honor his comical and sad goofs.

One website in particular (http://politicalhumor.about.com) host a list of Biden's Top 10 Gaffes by Daniel Kurtzman. Here are a few of the highlights:

- *"You cannot go to a 7-11 or a Dunkin' Donuts unless you have a slight Indian accent.... I'm not joking."* - Joe Biden casual conversation with Indian-American caught by C-SPAN June, 2006.

- *"I mean, you got the first mainstream African-American who is articulate and bright and clean and a nice-looking guy. I mean, that's a storybook, man."* - Joe Biden, describing Obama on January 31, 2007.

- *"A man I'm proud to call my friend. A man who will be the next President of the United States, Barack America!"* - Joe Biden, introducing Barack Obama at a campaign event in Springfield, Illinois on August 23, 2008.

- *"When the stock market crashed, Franklin D. Roosevelt got on the television and didn't just talk about the, you know, the princes of greed. He said, 'Look, here's what happened."* - Joe Biden in an interview with Katie Couric on September 22, 2008. Ooops!! FDR was NOT president during the stock market crashed and only experimental TV sets were in use at that time.

- *"Look, John's last-minute economic plan does nothing to tackle the number-one job facing the middle class, and it happens to be, as Barack says, a three-letter word: jobs. J-O-B-S, jobs."* - Joe Biden on the campaign trail in Athens, Ohio, October 15, 2008. He can't count but at least he spelled it correctly.

51. Obama has visited all 57 states

During a campaign event in Beaverton, Oregon, candidate Barack Obama added seven new states to our union.

"It is wonderful to be back in Oregon…Over the last 15 months, we've traveled to every corner of the United States. I've now been in 57 states? I think one left to go. Alaska and Hawaii, I was not allowed to go to even though I really wanted to visit, but my staff would not justify it."[lxiv]

The mainstream media quickly chalked it up to the candidate being tired. It is safe to say the media's treatment would not have been the same had the remark come from Sarah Palin, George Bush or another Republican.

Rush Limbaugh had a different take alluding to what might have been a Freudian slip.

> *"I mean, Dan Quayle goes out there and misspells potato, and we still get jokes about it. Barack Obama says he's gonna go out and campaign in 57 states, he was just tired, you know, it's been such a long campaign, he's been so many places, he probably thinks there are 57 states. Well, I have here a printout from a website called the International Humanist and Ethical Union. And here is how the second paragraph of an article on that website begins. "Every year from 1999 to 2005 the organization of the Islamic conference representing the 57 Islamic states presented a resolution to the United Nations commission on human rights called combating --""* – Rush Limbaugh, May 12, 2008.[lxv]

52. He has already won the Nobel Prize. There are no more fake honors to give him.

In 2009 President Obama won the Nobel Peace Prize. This was a very surprising choice from the Nobel Prize committee because Obama truly had no record of accomplishment that would lead one to believe him qualified to be nominated nonetheless win the prize.

Obama even said so himself in a Rose Garden address - "I am most surprised and deeply humbled… I do not view it as a recognition of my own accomplishments…I do not feel that I deserve to be in the company of so many transformative figures that have been honored by this prize."

The prize committee said it had decided to honor Obama because of his initiatives to reduce nuclear arms and to reduce tensions with the Muslim world. In other words they were granting the award which is usually reserved for individuals with a life time of work in the area of peace on a few campaign promises. The February 1 deadline for Obama's nomination was less than two weeks after his inauguration hardly any time to have an impact as President.

Prior to taking the oath of office, Obama served a portion of a term in the U.S. Senate as the junior Senator from Illinois during which he spent most of the time campaigning for president. Prior to that he was in the Illinois Legislature where he voted present over 125 times[lxvi] and before that was a community organizer. This resume hardly qualifies for the award but since he's already won, it is time for him to go.

53. Calling all snitches – Obama turning us against ourselves

In one of the most blatantly political moves ever to come out of the White House the Obama Administration asked online web surfers to turn in fellow web surfers and bloggers if they posted or wrote anything that goes against the Obama agenda. This email snitching scandal was thought to go too far for even a political party but coming directly from the White House was outrageous.

Specifically, the White House asked supporters to email any "fishy" information seen on the internet or via email to flag@whitehouse.gov.

The American Center for Law and Justice called on Obama to repudiate this effort. Jay Sekulow the group's chief counsel, told Fox News "This is a very troubling attempt to stifle the free speech of Americans who have the Constitutional right to express their opinion and concerns... And, worse, it turns the White House into some sort of self-appointed 'speech police.' This new White House reporting program strikes at the heart of the First Amendment."[lxvii]

The ACLU weighed in saying the White House effort is a "bad idea that could send a troublesome message."

Senator John Cornyn (R-TX), raised questions about what the Administration was doing with the names collected and called on Obama to end the program.

54. The Reader-in-Chief - going where no teleprompter has gone before

Obama's reliance on the teleprompter has become one of the very symbols of his presidency. Apparently the "eloquent one" is not quite as eloquent when not reading directly from a prepared script and perhaps his agenda is so far-fetched that when speaking freely he is liable to counter his own radical agenda with some commonsense remarks.

Even Jon Stewart of the *Daily Show* has criticized Obama for his incessant use of the teleprompter including an event before a small class of sixth graders at Graham Road Elementary School in Falls Church, VA.

Another one of the more bizarre examples pointed out by the *Washington Examiner* was when Obama required two teleprompters for a three-minute speech that is mostly pomp and circumstance when he nominated Alan Krueger to serve as chairman of his Council of Economic Advisers.

55. Obama's wife wants to take away my Big Mac and fries and my kid's Happy Meal.

Michelle Obama has declared war on American fast food and in particular the beloved French fry. She declares this war on freedom at the same time cities like San Francisco are attempting to ban toys in kid's meals.

Anyone wanting to ban the kid's meal toy has obviously never needed a small distraction while taking a long car trip with kids to visit the in-laws. First they mandate that everyone must purchase their government run healthcare and now they want to dictate what we can eat.

America is supposed to be the land of the free.

.

CHAPTER 8

The Failed Obama Economy

There are two distinct classes of men - those who pay taxes and those who receive and live upon taxes.
- Thomas Paine

56. America cannot afford four more years of Obama

Obama is spending America into oblivion. In just his first year in office our national deficit tripled. Standard & Poor's dropped our national credit rating for the first time in history. Our national debt has now surpassed $15 trillion dollars. We literally cannot afford another four years of Obama in the White House.

The Blaze ran an article that pointed out the "Obama increased national debt more in 4 days than Truman and Eisenhower did in 10 years."[lxviii]

57. Obama refuses to take responsibility for anything. Blaming Bush is not a leadership strategy.

It has been almost three years since President Obama took office, yet he still blames Bush for everything the American voter could conceive as wrong with the country. Let us not forget Obama not Bush tripled the national deficit in his first year in office. Obama not Bush shoved Obamacare down the throats of the American public. Obama not Bush is the President and has been for nearly three years.

The blame game might work in elementary school student council elections but the American public will not tolerate it from the highest office in the land.

58. National unemployment rate

According to the Bureau of Labor Statistics the national unemployment rate currently sits at 9 percent.[lxix] This represents a nearly two point increase since Obama took office despite repeated claims that government bailouts and massive "stimulus" spending would keep unemployment rates low.

59. Jobs lost since taking office

In January 2009, When Obama took the oath of office 133.5 million Americans were working in non-farm jobs according to the Bureau of Labor Statistics. On November 4, 2011 one year before the presidential election the Bureau reported that number to be 131 million. This represents a net loss of more than 2 million American jobs on Obama's watch.[lxx]

60. Unemployment rates in the states

Since taking office, President Obama has seen unemployment rates increase in 45 states and the District of Columbia. [lxxi]

Ten states including: California (11.9), Florida (10.6), Georgia (10.3), Illinois (10.0), Michigan (11.1), Mississippi (10.6), Nevada (13.4), North Carolina (10.5), Rhode Island (10.5), South Carolina (11.0). Additionally the District of Columbia is experiencing an unemployment rate of 11.1% and Puerto Rico has a whopping 15.1%.

State	Jan-09	Sep-11	Percent Increase/ Decrease	State	Jan-09	Sep-11	Percent Increase/ Decrease
Alabama	7.8	9.8	2	Montana	5.6	7.7	2.1
Alaska	7	7.6	0.6	Nebraska	4.1	4.2	0.1
Arizona	8.2	9.1	0.9	Nevada	9.9	13.4	3.5
Arkansas	6.6	8.3	1.7	New Hampshire	5.2	5.4	0.2
California	9.7	11.9	2.2	New Jersey	7.5	9.2	1.7
Colorado	6.8	8.3	1.5	New Mexico	5.8	6.6	0.8
Connecticut	7.1	8.9	1.8	New York	7.1	8	0.9
Delaware	7	8.1	1.1	North Carolina	9.2	10.5	1.3
District of Columbia	8.3	11.1	2.8	North Dakota	3.9	3.5	-0.4
Florida	8.5	10.6	2.1	Ohio	8.6	9.1	0.5
Georgia	8.5	10.3	1.8	Oklahoma	5.1	5.9	0.8
Hawaii	6	6.4	0.4	Oregon	9.9	9.6	-0.3
Idaho	6.4	9	2.6	Pennsylvania	6.8	8.3	1.5
Illinois	8.1	10	1.9	Rhode Island	9.6	10.5	0.9
Indiana	9	8.9	-0.1	South Carolina	9.9	11	1.1
Iowa	5.1	6	0.9	South Dakota	4.3	4.6	0.3
Kansas	5.8	6.7	0.9	Tennessee	9	9.8	0.8
Kentucky	9.2	9.7	0.5	Texas	6.4	8.5	2.1
Louisiana	5.6	6.9	1.3	Utah	5.8	7.4	1.6
Maine	7.4	7.5	0.1	Vermont	6.2	5.8	-0.4
Maryland	6.2	7.4	1.2	Virginia	5.7	6.5	0.8
Massachusetts	7.1	7.3	0.2	Washington	7.7	9.1	1.4
Michigan	11.3	11.1	-0.2	West Virginia	5.7	8.2	2.5
Minnesota	7.3	6.9	-0.4	Wisconsin	7.2	7.8	0.6
Mississippi	8.2	10.6	2.4	Wyoming	4.4	5.8	1.4
Missouri	8	8.7	0.7	US National	7.2	9	1.8

Source: U.S. Department of Labor, Bureau of Labor Statistics

61. Even Obama says he should be a one termer

Less than one month after taking office, President Obama made an appearance on the *Today Show* to pitch his plan to turn around the economy and create jobs.

Matt Lauer asked him about the consequences for his presidency if he failed to turn things around and Obama replied "I will be held accountable… If I don't have this done in three years, then there's going to be a one-term proposition."

When Obama made that statement the national unemployment rate was 7.6 percent.

Three years later the unemployment rate still hovers above 9 percent a far cry from a turnaround and what should definitely be a "one term" proposition.[lxxii]

62. Obama gets another first – The S&P dropped the Nation's credit rating

For the first time ever the United States lost its sterling credit rating from Standard & Poor's. This rating was granted to the U.S. 94 years ago in 1917 but on Friday, August 5, 2011 the credit rating agency dropped triple AAA rating to AA-plus. The Administration was warned about the potential for this move back in in April but it obviously fell on deaf ears.[lxxiii]

Instead of addressing the nation's $15 trillion debt problem and getting serious about tightening the belt on discretionary spending and entitlement spending, the Administration attacked members of Congress that put spending cut proposals forward. This debate peaked during the battle over the nation's debt ceiling, a spending barrier imposed by Congress to limit how much the government can borrow. To no one's surprise the

Administration steamrolled Congress and got another $2.1 trillion to spend.[lxxiv]

In addition to this downgrade, the S&P issued a negative outlook for the U.S. which is a warning that it might lower the rating again over the next two years.

Will Congress act? Not with the spendoholic Obama at the helm.

63. Obama waves goodbye to our last stable rating

On November 28, 2011 the U.S. lost the final stable rating from the big three credit rating agencies. Fitch Ratings reported that it will keep its rating for long-term U.S. debt at the AAA level, but is "lowering its outlook to negative."

John Detrixhe with Bloomberg News reported, "Fitch's outlook on the US, which it still assigns its top AAA grade, reflects 'declining confidence that timely fiscal measures necessary to place US public finances on a sustainable path will be forthcoming,' making the probability of a downgrade greater than 50 percent over two years."[lxxv]

CNN's Erin Burnett said Fitch's announcement was *"expected, but is another reminder of the failure in Washington."[lxxvi]*

64. He is crushing American Business with New regulations

The Obama Administration saddled American businesses with 132 "economically significant" new rules and regulations during the first two years of their reign. This represents a 40% higher rate of government intrusion than under Presidents Bill Clinton or George W. Bush.[lxxvii]

In addition to the new rules, regulators have hit U.S. employers with a 167% increase in violation fines and penalties.[lxxviii]

We are experiencing the hardest economic environment in decades yet the Obama Administration has made the conscious decision to pile the burden of excessive regulation on the back of the very businesses that could hire, innovate and get our economy running again.

The Heritage Foundation released a report, *Red Tape Rising*, over the summer of 2011 in which they noted: "Overall, from the beginning of the Obama Administration to mid-FY 2011, regulators have imposed $38 billion in new costs on the American people, more than any comparable period on record.

65. Shovel ready was a shovel load of something... just not jobs

Obama successfully duped Congress and some of the American public into supporting and passing the $787 billion "Stimulus" bill (The American Reinvestment Act) because he said it would put Americans back to work by funding "shovel ready" jobs. After passage of the monstrous spending bill it became very clear very quickly that "shovel ready" was just another lie used as a political ploy to expand government control and had nothing to do with putting Americans back to work.

The term "shovel ready" became the butt of late night jokes and a national symbol of inefficient, corrupt government spending.

The Inspector General of the Department of Energy, Gregory Friedman stated in testimony before the House Oversight and Government Reform Committee that bureaucratic hurdles among other things prevented the Energy Department from creating the promised number of jobs from the $35.2 billion allotted to the Department by the stimulus bill.

Friedman stated: "The concept of 'shovel-ready' projects was not realized, nor, as we now have confirmed, was it a realistic expectation."

Obama has even admitted so himself when at a meeting of his jobs and competitive council in Durham, North Carolina he stated "Shovel-ready was not as shovel-ready as we expected."[lxxix] This realization did not stop the Obama Administration from spending the taxpayers $787 billion and coming back to Congress to ask for more.

66. Obama has a warped sense of how to create jobs.

Matt Cover with *CNSNews* reported that the American taxpayer was on the hook for a more than a whopping $225,000 dollars per job created or saved by Obama's stimulus bill which he signed on February 17, 2009.

Cover analyzed a report from the nonpartisan Congressional Budget Office in which it estimated the impact of the "stimulus" bill also known as the American Recovery and Reinvestment Act.

The CBO report increased the original estimated cost of the stimulus bill from $787 billion to $821 billion. The report also estimates that the maximum number of jobs that could have been created or saved by the spending bill to be 3.6 million. Once one does the math of dividing 3.6 million jobs by $821 billion the average cost per job to the American taxpayer is $228,055.[lxxx]

On November 15, 2011, Doug Elmendorf, Director of the Congressional Budget Office, testified before the Senate Budget Committee. In answering a question from Senator Jeff Sessions (R-AL) he revealed that the stimulus bill will actually be a "drag on GDP" for the next decade. Should legislation that will effectively shrink our economy's potential over a ten year period be called a stimulus?[lxxxi]

67. I want my light bulb back!

In cartoons a bright idea is symbolized by a "light bulb." Unfortunately the light bulb has now come to symbolize one of the dumbest ideas to come out of Washington and one that is fully supported by Barack Obama.

In a full blown flexing of the "nanny state" muscle in Washington, Congress outlawed the traditional incandescent light bulb. This brought about outrage from the American public and the House Republicans voted to repeal the new law in the spring of 2011.

President Obama would not accept this move by Republicans and sent his Secretary of Energy, Steven Chu out to defend the unpopular environmentalist law.

Mr. Chu defended the law stating that the newly required more-efficient bulbs would save American money over the life of the bulb countering the much higher up front cost. Apparently Mr. Chu doesn't have any rarely used bulbs that sit unused for the most part in a in a shed, attic closet, or odd lamp from the in-laws. In his mind and in Obama's all Americans including the poor should be forced to purchase the expensive light bulbs because it will appease their radical left wing base.

Many consumers complain that the new "efficient" light bulbs do not work as well as the good old fashion incandescent bulb and many Republicans and consumer groups have raised concerns about the amount of mercury in some of the new bulbs that can escape when the bulb breaks.

68. Obama is the Grinch that tried to steal Christmas trees

Obama turned into the Grinch that would steal Christmas in November 2011. His
Department of Agriculture announced that it would impose a new 15 cent tax on all fresh-cut Christmas trees.

It's bad enough that American families will celebrate Christmas this year during one of the worst economic environments in decades but Obama thought it would be worth squeezing out a little more government revenue by attacking the sale of Christmas trees.

The Heritage Foundation's David Addington explained in a report that the tax was to "support a new Federal program to improve the image and marketing of Christmas trees." Is this really the role of our federal government?

ABC News reported that that the special Christmas Tree tax was first announced in the Federal Registry on November 8 but the fee generated such a backlash that President Obama and the Department of Agriculture decided almost immediately to delay implementation until after the 2011 Christmas season.

69. Obama chooses class warfare over leadership

Obama has said time and time again that the rich do not pay their fair share of taxes and has proposed raising their taxes. This is simply not true. Ten percent of the U.S. taxpayers are currently bearing more that 70 percent of the total tax burden. How one can claim that lopsided burden is proof of shirking their responsibility is unfathomable. Obama's wealth redistribution agenda and desire to create a dependent class overshadows any hint of reality.

Just take a look at the average federal income tax burden paid by the top 10 percent of income earners over the last 5 tax years and compare it to the bottom 50 percent of income earners.

Tax Year	Percent of total federal income taxes paid by the Top 10 % of wage earners	Percent of total federal income taxes paid by the Bottom 50% of wage earners
2009	70.47	2.25
2008	69.94	2.7
2007	71.22	2.89
2006	70.79	2.99
2005	70.3	3.07
Average:	**70.544**	**2.78**

When looking at the facts it is hard to believe Obama can make such outlandish claims while keeping a straight face. Currently more than 47% of American households pay no federal income taxes. That's right zero. Does that seem fair?

70. There are actually 15 trillion reasons to defeat Obama

This list is a compilation of the 101 most compelling reasons to ensure that Barack Obama is a one-term president. In reality there are over 15 trillion reasons to oust Obama from office along with all of the other members of the political establishment that are spending our country into a financial crisis that we may not be able to recover from.

On November 16, 2011 our country's national debt surpassed $15 trillion dollars. That is over $48,000 of debt for every U.S. citizen or over $133,000 of debt for those of us that pay taxes. [lxxxii]

71. Obama's "green job" failures are destroying American jobs

The Obama Administration has been a series of green jobs failures that have cost the American taxpayers billions and set an environment of regulatory uncertainty that has hampered economic growth.

Obama's "green" handouts in the way of billions through taxpayer subsidized loans to failing companies such as Solyndra or Beacon Power while at the same time refusing to lift the drilling moratorium in the Gulf of Mexico or to approve the Keystone XL Pipeline is all one needs to know about Obama's desire to create jobs and spur economic growth. Worse yet, take a look at his plan to implement a cap-and-trade emission scheme that would cripple American businesses from competing in the global market place.

Whether it is the appointment of Van Jones as "Green Jobs Czar" or his failed "Cash for Caulkers" program it has been one failure after another that has hurt the American taxpayer and bruised the American economy.

A Department of Labor, a green jobs program that was scheduled to allocate 500 million of taxpayer dollars was such a failure that the Department's inspector general recommend that the bulk of the money be returned to the Treasury. The failed program was reported to have only successfully get 15 percent of participants into jobs.[lxxxiii]

72. Obama would make opening a coal plant impossible

As if there was any doubt about Obama's anti-jobs through energy destruction agenda he made it crystal clear in a January 2008 interview with the *San Francisco Chronicle* explaining his cap-and-trade vision.

Obama stated in reference to a question regarding coal, "So if somebody wants to build a coal-powered plant, they can it's just that it will bankrupt them because they're going to be charged a huge sum for all that greenhouse gas that's being emitted."

With comments like these there is no wonder the Obama economy has failed and why he refuse to lift the drilling moratorium in the Gulf of Mexico or approve the Keystone XL pipeline.

73. Eric Holder, Obama's Attorney General

If Obama is going to surround himself with incompetent people that are now in charge of running our government he must go.

Eric Holder, Obama's attorney General is responsible for the Fast and Furious gun running debacle. As Sarah Palin wrote in a *Fox Nation* post titled "Fire Holder Now": *Why would any government official with an ounce of common sense think it's a good idea to facilitate the smuggling of thousands of guns into the hands of violent Mexican drug cartels? That's what Operation Fast and Furious did.*[lxxxiv]

Eric Holder went after Arizona Governor Jan Brewer and the Arizona Immigration law publically even before he had the common courtesy to read the law. Is that the kind of knee jerk, politically driven reaction we want from our nation's top law enforcement officer?

Eric Holder is responsible for dismissing the open and closed case involving the Black Panther's voter intimidation activities in Philadelphia during the 2008 election. This was purely a political move and has no place from someone in this high position.

74. Obama calls Americans lazy

Instead of taking responsibility for his failed economy, Obama lashes out at all Americans and calls us soft, lazy and without a competitive edge. Apparently Obama realized that blaming Bush was losing traction so changed course and decided to attack the American worker.

"The way I think about it is, this is a great, great country that had gotten a little soft and we didn't have that same competitive edge that we needed over the last couple of decades." - Obama on September 29, 2011 interview with NBC's Jim Payne.

"The way I think about it is, this is a great, great country that had gotten a little soft and we didn't have that same competitive edge that we needed over the last couple of decades." - Remarks by President Obama at APEC CEO Business Summit, Honolulu, Hawaii, November 12, 2011

Mr. President- The American people are not lazy but we are getting sick and tired of your excessive anti-business regulation and continued chastisement. It is time for you to go.

75. Obama attacks the state of Arizona and lies about immigration

In 2010 the State of Arizona passed a law to crack down on illegal immigration in their state. Immediately the Obama Administration went down an unusual path of attacking state legislation from the White House. Never a fan of the States rights and the Tenth Amendment, Obama stood in the Rose Garden and chastised the new law as "misguided" and stated how it would "undermine the basic notions of fairness that we cherish as Americans."

The Administration and the Democrat attack dogs in the media, claimed that the new law would require racial profiling by Arizona law enforcement officials. In fact nothing could be further from the truth. As the Heritage Foundation's, Hans von Spakovsky points out in a October 2010 report:

Arizona state law actually contains more stringent restrictions against racial profiling than federal guidelines published by the U.S. Department of Justice (DOJ). Consequently, if the Obama Administration files suit alleging that the Arizona law is illegal because it uses racial profiling and is discriminatory, it will also have to file suit against all of the federal law enforcement agents who follow DOJ's Guidance on race profiling in law enforcement activities. Such a suit against Arizona is completely unwarranted and would constitute litigation based on political or other improper considerations, not the rule of law.

The Obama Administration directed the Department of Justice to examine the legislation and has filed a suit that is still pending against the new law.

76. Obama shunned his duty and refused to enter the spending debate

In August 2011, Congress created a bipartisan "Super Committee" that was tasked developing a plan to cut $1.2 trillion from the U.S. Debt by November 23, 2011. The committee was formed after Congress failed to come up with ways to cut the debt during the earlier debt ceiling fight.

For nearly four month the committee debated spending cuts and tax increases before failing to come up with a passable plan. During this time Obama was nowhere to be found. New Jersey Governor Chis Christie blasted the President for his total absence during a November 29, 2011 press conference: "We're left with an indecisive President who is more concerned about his public image and winning reelection than solving the nation's problems…. What the hell are we paying you for?"[lxxxv]

The committee's failure triggered an automatic cut of $1.2 trillion was automatically triggered. The brunt of this automatic cut will be felt by the Department of Defense and our men and women in uniform.

Obama is basing his re-election campaign on strategy of running against what he calls a "do nothing Congress." Too bad for him we all know he is a "do nothing" good for America President.

CHAPTER 9

Excessive Vacations during a Recession

You can't take a trip to Las Vegas or down to the Super Bowl on the taxpayers' dime.
-President Barack Obama

77. Michelle the Globe Trotter – A modern day Marie Antoinette

Michelle Obama has become known more for her jet setting ways than her domestic policy initiatives. Perhaps her most infamous trip came last summer when she and her entourage of 40 took a lavish European vacation in southern Spain.

It is important to remember that back home Americans were experiencing double digit unemployment rates. Many that were lucky enough to be employed were living paycheck to paycheck and a vacation was not even in the realm of possibility. That reality didn't stop Michelle from going in fact it might have spurred her on.

Andrea Tantaros, a *New York Daily News* columnist labeled the material girl Michelle Obama "the modern day Marie Antoinette." This vacation, which the Obama's described as a private mother-daughter trip (with 30+ friends and staff) took place at what is considered Spain's most exclusive hotel the Villa Padierna. At least 30 rooms were reserved for the Obama entourage.

The European press lampooned the Obamas for such an extravagant vacation during such tough economic times and for closing a public beach for their 40 member strong entourage. This four-day super vacation is rumored to have cost $375,000.[lxxxvi]

78. Bathing suits are more important that underwear bombs

On Christmas day 2009, the alleged Christmas Day bomber, Umar Farouk Abdulmutallab attempted to detonate plastic explosives hidden in his underwear while on board a Northwest Airlines flight from Amsterdam to Detroit.

Obama who was busy enjoying his Hawaiian vacation refused to interrupt his beach time to reassure the American public that this was an isolated incident and that our airways were safe. It isn't like the holidays are a busy travel time or anything.

Instead Obama continued to sun bathe and body surf while completely ignoring the situation. A full four days later the President finally succumbed to political pressure and made a public statement regarding the failed underwear bombing. [lxxxvii]

Leadership is not conveyed by ignoring one's duties.

79. Martha's Vineyard vacation – Double or Nothing

This summer the Obamas took an eleven day vacation to Martha's Vineyard. It isn't unusual for presidents to take some time off in August but the current economic environment puts a dark cloud around this vacation decision.

Many cash-strapped families across the country were foregoing a vacation again this year and staying home instead. Despite this reality, President Obama and his entourage went to Martha's Vineyard which cost the taxpayers millions.

One of the more peculiar twists in the first families travel plans is that they refused to coordinate their travel schedules (mind you the president and first lady have an entire office dedicated to planning their travel). This means the American taxpayer had to foot the bill for 2 separate trips to Martha's Vineyard and 2 separate trips from Martha's Vineyard.

Hello Mr. President, our country is drowning in debt. You constantly promote the notion of green jobs and reducing one's carbon footprint yet you can't coordinate travel with your wife – STRIKE THAT – because you won't have your taxpayer funded staff coordinate travel with your wife's taxpayer funded staff? Ridiculous!

80. We don't want a mulligan - We want a leader!

Obama has already hit the links 28 times in 2011 to play golf and 86 times since taking office.

While this would be excessive during any administration it is important to point out that we are currently experiencing the worst economy since the Great Depression and involved in two wars.lxxxviii

Perhaps instead of working on his handicap President Obama should be working on the unemployment rate and economy!

To put this into perspective, President George W. Bush only golfed 24 times over his entire eight years in office.

CHAPTER 10

Anti-Religious beliefs and actions

We hold these truths to be self-evident, that all men are created equal, that they are endowed by their Creator with certain unalienable Rights, that among these are Life, Liberty and the pursuit of Happiness.
- Declaration of Independence

81. Obama stopped the WWII Memorial Prayer Plaque

In an outrageous attempt to appease the radical anti-religious left the Obama Administration has objected to a plaque that would show President Roosevelt's prayer at the World War II Memorial in Washington, DC.

The Obama Administration stated that displaying Roosevelt's prayer would dilute the message of the memorial.[lxxxix]

The prayer in question is one in which President Roosevelt asked the nation to join him in prayer during a fireside chat as U.S. troops launched the D-day invasion to defeat Nazi Germany.

Obama may be able to temporarily block this prayer from the memorial that honors our fallen heroes and all who served in World War II, but once we vote him out of office this prayer can grace the walls of this precious American monument.

President Franklin D. Roosevelt, June 6, 1944:

Almighty God: Our sons, pride of our Nation, this day have set upon a mighty endeavor, a struggle to preserve our Republic, our religion, and our civilization, and to set free a suffering humanity.

Lead them straight and true; give strength to their arms, stoutness to their hearts, steadfastness in their faith.

They will need Thy blessings. Their road will be long and hard. For the enemy is strong. He may hurl back our forces. Success may not come with rushing speed, but we shall return again and again; and we know that by Thy grace, and by the righteousness of our cause, our sons will triumph.

They will be sore tried, by night and by day, without rest-until the victory is won. The darkness will be rent by noise and flame. Men's souls will be shaken with the violences of war.

For these men are lately drawn from the ways of peace. They fight not for the lust of conquest. They fight to end conquest. They fight to liberate. They fight to let justice arise, and tolerance and good will among all Thy people. They yearn but for the end of battle, for their return to the haven of home.

Some will never return. Embrace these, Father, and receive them, Thy heroic servants, into Thy kingdom.

And for us at home -- fathers, mothers, children, wives, sisters, and brothers of brave men overseas -- whose thoughts and prayers are ever with them--help us, Almighty God, to rededicate ourselves in renewed faith in Thee in this hour of great sacrifice.

Many people have urged that I call the Nation into a single day of special prayer. But because the road is long and the desire is great, I ask that our people devote themselves in a continuance of prayer. As we rise to each new day, and again when each day is spent, let words of prayer be on our lips, invoking Thy help to our efforts.

Give us strength, too -- strength in our daily tasks, to redouble the contributions we make in the physical and the material support of our armed forces.

And let our hearts be stout, to wait out the long travail, to bear sorrows that may come, to impart our courage unto our sons where ever they may be.

And, O Lord, give us Faith. Give us Faith in Thee; Faith in our sons; Faith in each other; Faith in our united crusade. Let not the keenness of our spirit ever be dulled. Let not the impacts of temporary events, of temporal matters of but fleeting moment let not these deter us in our unconquerable purpose.

With Thy blessing, we shall prevail over the unholy forces of our enemy. Help us to conquer the apostles of greed and racial arrogancies. Lead us to the saving of our country, and with our sister Nations into a world unity that will spell a sure peace a peace invulnerable to the schemings of unworthy men. And a peace that will let all of men live in freedom, reaping the just rewards of their honest toil.

Thy will be done, Almighty God.

Amen.

82. Obama insults a majority of Americans on the Ground Zero Mosque

In the summer of 2009, the nation became outraged by an ongoing effort to build a Muslim community center and mosque just yards away from "Ground Zero" the site of the World Trade Centers that were attacked on September 11, 2001 by radical Muslim terrorists.

Given the extreme emotion and vivid memories of death and heroism that will forever be tied to this site, the proposed mosque was deemed very inappropriate and hurtful in the public's eye. President Obama in a constant need for attention and constant need to tell Americans they are wrong came out and strongly defended the proposed mosque at a White House dinner celebrating Ramadan.

Obama weighed into the issue, which legally must be handled at the local zoning level, by declaring "as a citizen, and as president, I believe that Muslims have the same right to practice their religion as anyone else in this country.... I understand the emotions that this issue engenders. Ground Zero is, indeed, hallowed ground…This is America, and our commitment to religious freedom must be unshakable."

83. Obama has the nerve to cover Jesus at Georgetown University, a Catholic school.

On April 14, 2009 President Obama spoke at Georgetown University. The White House only agreed to participate in the speech after all religious symbols, such as crosses, pictures of Jesus or Mary or other religious signage be covered up where the President was to speak.

The Catholic school granted the President's request so the speech could take place.

After the removal of religion request from the White House was made public, Bill Donohue , president of the Catholic League, addressed to the issue stating:

"The cowardice of Georgetown to stand fast on principle tells us more than we need to know about what is going on there, but the bigger story is the audacity of the Obama Administration to ask a religious school to neuter itself before the president speaks there.

"No bishop who might speak at the White House would ever request that a crucifix be displayed behind him. Moreover, the same church and state fanatics who go nuts every time a polling place is set up in the basement of a Catholic school have been noticeably silent over this incident "

The anti-religious left would be happy to to strike "under God" from the Pledge of Allegiance and dismiss Americas Judeo-Christian foundation. It is important to stand up for religious freedom and fight their anti-religion efforts.

Mr. President- Please read the Declaration of Independence.

84. Obama can't hide his anti- Israel beliefs

Obama would say that he is nothing but "pro-Israel" but his actions and the actions of Jewish voters would tell a different story.

Obama's strong stance against Israel has started to take its political toll on his re-election chances and on all Democrats that rely heavily on the usually strong Democrat block of Jewish voters.

In fact Obama's growing dislike and mistrust among Jewish voters led to Republican Bob Turner winning the heavily Jewish and reliably Democratic 9th Congressional District in the heart of New York City. This is a district where Democrats enjoy a 3 to 1 advantage among voters.

Jewish voters continue to flee Obama and rightly so. He has been cold to our critical ally Israel since taking office and has been outright hostile to Benjamin Netanyahu, the Israeli Prime Minister.

Obama has stated that Israel should adopt its pre-1967 borders that are indefensible because they are based on an armistice line and not a real border. Given the political and religious tensions in this area of the world an "indefensible" border is absurd.

Philip Kline with the *Washington Examiner* reported that "Obama decided that Jews building homes outside of Jerusalem was the biggest threat to Middle East peace - bigger than a nuclear Iran and certainly more significant than Palestinian terrorism - and demanded that Jews freeze construction there."

Additionally President Obama refused to condemn the Palestinian Authority President Mahmoud Abbas' plans to form a unity government with Hamas a terrorist group dedicated to the destruction of Israel.

Obama refused to weigh in when Abbas went before the United Nations General Assembly to ask for the ability for Palestine to unilaterally declare statehood without any peace deal with Israel.

In another embarrassing poke in the eye of one of our most important allies, Obama was caught on an open microphone speaking to French President Nicolas Sarkozy.

Sarkozy told Obama, "Netanyahu, I can't stand him. He's a liar" to which the anti-Israel Obama replied "You are sick of him, but I have to work with him every day."[xc] Oooops!

85. Obama mocks religion and calls Americans bitter

Obama showed his true colors by revealing his deep disdain for everything that has made America the greatest nation in history. At an elitist, wine and cheese event, Obama explained the problem with hardworking Pennsylvania and Midwest voters.

"And it's not surprising then that they get bitter, they cling to guns or religion or antipathy to people who aren't like them or anti-immigrant sentiment or anti-trade sentiment as a way to explain their frustrations…"

Obama's remarks removed some of smoke screen that the liberal media surrounded their chosen one with. It provided a rare glimpse into the mind of the most anti-religion, anti-gun, anti-military, anti-business president in American history.

CHAPTER 11

Obama's Failures are America's Failures

You never want a serious crisis to go to waste.
-Rahm Emanuel, Obama's former Chief of Staff

86. Arming the Drug Cartels and lying about it.

The Obama Administration has knowingly allowed and even facilitated the flow of weapons to the Mexican drug cartels. The now infamous program dubbed "Fast and Furious" was set up as a federal gun trafficking sting operation that was severely botched and allowed thousands of guns to walk into the hands of the cartels. These weapons are now responsible for at least two separate occasions where U.S. Agents were shot and killed.

Customs Enforcement Agent Jaime Zapata, was killed in a drug cartel ambush on a northern Mexican highway with a gun that was purchased outside Forth Worth as part of the botched Fast and Furious sting operation. Brian Terry a U.S. Border Patrol agent was shot and killed near Rio Rico, Arizona while trying to arrest a group of suspects. Two guns found at this murder scene were linked to the Fast and Furious operation.

Congressman Darryl Issa (R-CA), chairman of the House
Oversight and Government Reform Committee has launched an
investigation into the Fast and Furious project and subpoenaed
documents from Attorney General Eric Holder in an attempt to
find out how this outrageous program could have been authorized
to begin with and why Holder would not have stopped it
immediately.

Congressman Issa, Senator John Cornyn (R-TX) and Senator
Chuck Grassley (R-IA) among others have said that Holder
knowingly misled Congress in May 2009 when he stated under
oath that he first learned of Fast and Furious' gun-walking tactics
"over the last few weeks." In a Senate hearing held the first week
of November 2011, Holder admitted that his timeline might have
been off but refused to admit that he knew much about the
operation. He declared that memos referencing the detail of the
project never made it to his desk but were instead intercepted and
handled by his staff.

87. Obama ignores Gulf to Golf during largest oil spill in history

On April 20, 2010 the Deepwater Horizon, a BP run oil rig in the
Gulf of Mexico, had an explosion that killed 11 men and caused
an oil spill that gushed for 3 months and was not fully sealed for
5 months. This disaster is said to be the largest accidental marine
spill in the history of the petroleum industry. Roughly 53,000
barrels of oil leaked out of the ocean floor each day and a total of
nearly 50 million total barrels escaped endangering the Gulf
Coast.[xci]

Despite the sheer magnitude of this disaster Obama downplayed
the significance of the environmental catastrophe unfolding
before America's eyes. Obama was blatantly absent and
displayed absolutely no sense of leadership or urgency
throughout the entire ordeal. His lack of leadership was so

apparent that normally loyal members of his own political party were even attacking his lack of action. Democrat political strategist James Carville slammed Obama's response as "political stupidity" and told ABCs Good Morning America "I have no idea of why their attitude was so hands off here."[xcii]

Many political insiders compared this disaster and Obamas approach as "his Katrina" referring to President Bush and his Administration's response to the aftermath of the deadly Hurricane.
In an interview with Sean Hannity, former New York Mayor Rudy Giuliani said about Obama's response:

"It couldn't be worse. This would be an example, if you are taught leadership 101 of exactly what not to do. Minimize it at first. Two days after or three days after it happened, go on vacation. He's been on vacation more often than he has by far been to Louisiana or Mississippi or any of the places affected."

Obama's reaction to the disaster was so bad it took him 58 days to reach out and meet with executives from BP. Fifty eight days! What was our president doing during this time? Take a look for yourself:

- Day 4 Obama goes golfing in Asheville, NC
- Day 5 More golfing
- Day 8 Photo op with Yankees
- Day 10 High dollar fundraiser in Washington
- Day 11 Meeting with Rock star Bono at White House
- Day 19 Anther round of golf – the third since the oil well exploded
- Day 26 Another round of golf
- Day 33 More golf
- Day 37 Fundraiser for Senator Barbara Boxer (D-CA)
- Day 38 Takes family on a weekend vacation to Chicago
- Day 44 Attends Paul McCartney concert
- Day 48 Another concert this time by Kelly Clarkson

- Day 57 Goes golfing for sixth time since the Gulf disaster began.

(This list was largely complied from a column posted by Kevin Kristy on Politipage.com)

Obama's lackadaisical approach to biggest environmental disaster in recent time is truly unbelievable. These are not actions of a president.

88. No budget no worries – Obama has never been afraid to hide behind inaction

The Obama White House and Democrats on Capitol Hill have not submitted a budget since the fiscal 2010 budget was passed on April 3, 2009. That is 33 months, nearly 1,000 days and don't expect one anytime soon. The have made plenty of vitriolic speeches and platitudes but they have refused to put pen to paper and craft a budget.

This is a prime example of the abysmal leadership oozing from the White House. Obama flat out refuses to get our nation's financial house in order during an economic recession and during a time of unparalleled debt. Perhaps this should come as no surprise from the former Illinois State Senator that proudly voted "present" over 125 times because he was too scared or too unprincipled to take a stand.[xciii]

89. No gold medal for Obama

Despite the warnings from many political insiders and foreign relation experts Obama attempted to ride his perceived worldwide popularity and power to Copenhagen Denmark to pitch the International Olympic delegates (IOC) on Chicago's bid to host the 20016 Olympic Games. Needless to say it didn't go so well. I guess Obama's three continents 100 day American apology tour wasn't enough.

The *UK Times Online* reported that "Obama was humiliated by his failed pitch to use his 'Rock Star' persona to win the 2016 hosting of the Olympic Games in his home town of Chicago."

At the time Obama decided to enter the fray, he was being questioned whether a defeat could further tarnish his reputation both domestically and abroad. It wasn't just the defeat that sat in peoples mind after the results were made public. It was the overwhelming magnitude of Obama's defeat. Chicago was eliminated in the first round by a landslide vote of 18 yes to 94 no.

90. Obama lets the Space Shuttle program end with no plan for the future

On July 21, 2011 the Space Shuttle Atlantis landed safely at NASA's Kennedy Space Center in Florida for the last time. This landing marked the end of almost 30 years of the space shuttle program flights and the end of nearly 5 decades of America leading the world in space exploration.

Congressman Rob Bishop (R-UT) wrote a piece for the *Washington Examiner* titled "With end of Space Shuttle program, America now must depend on Russian taxis to get to space." Bishop opined *"While some Obama administration officials claim that the United States still has an 'active' manned space flight program, the reality is that we do not. To make this claim is a misrepresentation of the facts. For the first time in nearly 50 years, our country does not have the ability to put a human into space."*[xciv]

Texas Governor Rick Perry issued a press release stating *"Unfortunately, with the final landing of the Shuttle Atlantis and no indication of plans for future missions, this administration has set a significantly different milestone by shutting down our nation's legacy of leadership in human spaceflight and exploration.*"[xcv]

America's space shuttle program was the perfect example of American exceptionalism. We need a president who recognizes and embraces America's greatness.

91. Lied about closing Gitmo

Obama claimed on the campaign trail and during his first days in office that he would close the Guantanamo Bay detention facility. On January 22, 2009, he signed an Executive Order that would require Gitmo to be closed within a year.

Nearly three years later Gitmo is still up and running. This is actually a good promise for Obama to break. While keeping Gitmo up and running is a good thing this issue made the 101 list because Obama's efforts to close the facility and his incessant bad mouthing the facility both domestically and abroad have been a huge distraction in the war on terror. The fact he promised the world it would be closed it is just another Obama failure.

92. Rejections of Obama's policies led to a historic mid-term election

On November 2, 2010 the American people delivered a message loud and clear to President Obama – We do not agree with or support your radical transformation of America.

The historic mid-term election of 2010 was the biggest election swing that America has seen in over half a century. President Obama even admitted so calling the results a "shellacking."[xcvi]

In an interview on PBS, Michael Beschloss a presidential historian said it *"was historic for a couple of reasons. One is, the Obama presidency is unlikely to be the same again. The things he was able to do with control of Congress, it is going to be very different now that he's lost one house. Also, you don't usually see a wave of this magnitude, hasn't happened quite like this in at least a half-century. So, the American people were obviously saying something very powerful, very different from what they said two years ago."*[xcvii]

Republicans took control of the U.S. House of Representatives that day by gaining 60 seats. Additionally they gained 7 seats in the U.S. Senate and used the momentum to pick up 7 new governorships.[xcviii]

CHAPTER 12

Obama is Embarrassed of America – The Feeling is mutual.

And I'm proud to be an American,
where at least I know I'm free.
And I won't forget the men who died,
who gave that right to me.
And I gladly stand up,
next to you and defend Her still today.
Cause there ain't no doubt I love this land,
God bless the USA.

- Lee Greenwood, lyrics to "Proud to be an American"

93. Apologizing for Americas Greatness

Shortly after taking office Obama went on a worldwide apology tour confessing to anyone who would listen to his perceived sins of America and divulging his personal embarrassment of America's exceptionalism.

In less than 100 days he changed the world's perception of America from one of leadership and goodwill to one of failed leadership and pompous ineptitude. Obama hoped that by blaming America for all that is wrong in the world and furthermore placing blame on all of his "less wise" predecessors he would befriend our enemies and make America safer and stronger. This isn't the time of "hope" America voted for in 2008.

Karl Rove might have put it best in his *Wall Street Journal* commentary, A President Apology Tour - "A superstar, not a statesman, today leads our country. That may win short-term applause from foreign audiences, but do little for what should be the chief foreign policy preoccupation of any U.S. president: advancing America's long-term interests."

94. Apologizes and undermines the War on Terror

Obama uses a May 21, 2009 speech in Washington, DC to dismiss the War on Terror and label it a mistake made on hasty decisions that were based on fear.

> *"Our government made a series of hasty decisions. I believe that many of these decisions were motivated by a sincere desire to protect the American people. But I also believe that all too often our government made decisions based on fear rather than foresight, that all too often our government trimmed facts and evidence to fit ideological predispositions."* – Barack Obama, May 21, 2009

Our men and women in uniform deserve better and all victims of terrorism around the world deserve better.

95. Obama Believes America is Guilty of Snubbing Europe

Obama feels that America is arrogant and at fault for not acknowledging the entire continent of Europe's leadership role in the world.

> *"In America, there's a failure to appreciate Europe's leading role in the world. Instead of celebrating your dynamic union ... there have been times where America has shown arrogance and been dismissive, even derisive."*
> - Barack Obama speaking in Strasbourg, France, April 3, 2009

96. Obama attacks America for Gitmo

Obama can't pass up an opportunity to put America down and his favorite whipping boy seems to be Guantanamo. Obama likes to tell the world how bad we are and how bad the prison is at Guantanamo Bay. Nevermind the fact that the accommodations would be considered beyond luxury at any other high security prison in the world.

Obama is so set on belittling America. He doesn't seem to care that his own claims of American guilt can be used as recruiting tools by al Qaeda and other terrorist groups.

> *"In dealing with terrorism, we can't lose sight of our values and who we are. That's why I closed Guantanamo. That's why I made very clear that we will not engage in certain interrogation practices. I don't believe that there is a contradiction between our security and our values."* -
> Barack Obama speaking in Strasbourg, France, April 3, 2009

97. Obama would never pass up an opportunity to bad mouth America

Never passing up a chance to criticize the good ol' U.S.A when abroad, Obama used his November 2011 trip to Australia to dump on American school children. He told a classroom of Aussie students at Campbell High School that their counterparts in America had "fallen behind" when it comes to math and science education.[xcix]

Obama went further to say his administration is working to reform the public school system.

Keith Koffler editor of the White House Dossier, aptly points out that "*Obama might have thought twice before casting America's public school kids in a negative light to foreign students. Especially since he can exclude his own children from the system by paying for them to attend private school.*"

Sidwell Friends the school the Obama's chose to send their children is reported to cost $33,000 a year.

98. Obama sees America as a Dark even evil place.

Obama just can't get his head around the fact that America is great. Instead he must dwell on issues hundreds of years old and spout them to the world in an effort to make himself seem more compassionate. He claims we are working through dark times and in a way he is right – his presidency and failed economy.

> "*The United States is still working through some of our own darker periods in our history…. Our country still struggles with the legacies of slavery and segregation, the*

past treatment of Native American." - Barack Obama speaking before the Turkish Parliament on April 6 2009.

99. America at Fault in Muslim Relationship

Obama took the opportunity during an interview with Al Arabiya to criticize the U.S. instead of confronting radical Muslims that have launched a terrorist Jihad against Christians and the west.

"My job to the Muslim world is to communicate that the Americans are not your enemy. We sometimes make mistakes. We have not been perfect."
- Obama on Al Arabiya, January 27, 2009.

100. Michelle Obama was never proud to be an American

This one is an oldie but goodie. Just read Michelle's words that she said not once but twice in one day at two separate campaign events in Wisconsin in 2008.

"for the first time in my adult life I am proud of my country" – Michelle Obama speaking in Milwaukee, Wisconsin.

"For the first time in my adult lifetime, I'm really proud of my country, and not just because Barack has done well, but because I think people are hungry for change." - Michelle Obama speaking later that day in Madison, Wisconsin.

These outrageous statements say all anyone needs to know about Michelle or Barack Obama and explains his complete embarrassment of and denial of American exceptionalism. It puts into perspective how the first couple could sit through years of anti-American sermons by the Reverend Jeremiah Wright. It

explains his desire have a "radical transformation of America."
And it explains his worldwide apology tour.

America deserves a president who is proud of America.

101. Obama is surrounded by tax cheats

President Obama has time and time again tried to sell the
American people on tax increases and consistently says that the
rich don't pay their fair share.

Obama should take a closer look at the people he surrounds
himself with before he starts accusing the public of shirking their
tax duty. Obama has surrounded himself with tax cheats.

The Washington Times highlighted some of the higher profile tax
problems facing the Administration in an April 2009 Editorial:

- *Kathleen Sebelius, Obama's Secretary of Health and
  Human Resources and her husband recently paid $7,040
  in back taxes and $878 dollars in interest and penalties
  for minor amendments to their 2005-2007 tax returns.*

- *First HHS Secretary nominee and former Democratic
  Sen. Tom Daschle of South Dakota who filed over
  $140,000 in back taxes and interest in January after
  failing to disclose more than $300,000 in income,
  including the use of a car and driver. His violations of the
  tax code remain the most impressive and lead to his
  removing his name for consideration.*

- *Treasury Secretary Timothy Geithner failed to pay more
  than $40,000 in payroll taxes when he worked for the
  International Monetary Fund, correcting the error before
  the Senate voted on his nomination.*

- *The husband of Labor Secretary Hilda Solis paid around $6,400 prior to her nomination vote for tax liens on his Los Angeles auto repair business dating from 1993. The White House said Ms. Solis and her husband were unaware of the lien.*

- *Chief Performance Officer nominee Nancy Killefer withdrew her nomination in the wake of the Daschle tax disclosures after it came to light that she had a $947 tax lien filed against her by the District of Columbia in 2005 for failing to pay compensation taxes for a domestic employee. District records show she owed $298 in unemployment compensation, $48.69 in interest, and $600.00 in penalties that she paid five months later.*

(From *Washington Times* editorial "Obama's 'taxing' nominees" April 3, 2009)

[i] http://www.cbo.gov/ftpdocs/107xx/doc10781/11-30-premiums.pdf

[ii] http://cbo.gov/ftpdocs/115xx/doc11579/06-30-LTBO.pdf

[iii] *Human Events*, "President Obama is becoming a veritable Pinocchio by stretching the truth on a regular basis..." July 23, 2011

[iv] *New York Times*, "Book Challenges Obama on Mother's Deathbed Fight," by Kevin Sack, July 13, 2011

[v] www.mckinsey.com, "Employer Survey on US Health care Reform: Details regarding the survey methodology" June 2011

[vi] *Newsmax*, "Joe Wilson: I Was Right to Yell 'You Lie' at Obama", August 17, 2011

[vii] Foxnews.com, Issa Eyes Political Connections That Drove Loan Approvals Like Solyndra, October 09, 2011

[viii] Fox News Channel, Special Report with Brett Baird, November 9, 2011

[ix] Foxnews.com, Issa Eyes Political Connections That Drove Loan Approvals Like Solyndra, October 09, 2011

[x] *The Daily Caller*, Financial turmoil grips two more 'green energy' companies receiving federal loan guarantees, By Jim Davis October, 31 2011

[xi] *New York Post*, LightSquared: Putting O's donors first?, By Michelle Malkin, September 23, 2011

[xii] *Los Angeles Times*, "Cost, need questioned in $433-million smallpox drug deal", by David Willman, November 13, 2011

[xiii] *Forbes*, "Is Bizarre Smallpox Drug Deal Obama Administration's Next Solyndra?" By Rick Ungar, November 13, 2011.

[xiv] *Politico*, "Sestak confirms WH job offer to get out of Senate race," May 23, 2010

[xv] *Politico*, "Sestak confirms WH job offer to get out of Senate race," May 23, 2010

[xvi] *News Busters*, "Denver Post Goes Silent on Senate Candidate

Job Offer Scandal,"
by P.J. Gladnick, May 27, 2010
[xvii] MVPProject.org, "Military Voting in 2010:A Step Forward, But A Long Way To Go," by Eric Eversole

[xix] *The Washington Times,* "At the President's Pleasure" by The Washington Times, Editorial, September 28, 2009.

[xx] Fox News, "Obama's Science Czar Considered Forced Abortions, Sterilization as Population Growth Solutions", by Joseph Abrams, Published July 21, 2009

[xxi] *NewsMax,* "White House Science Czar Involved in Climategate" by L.D. Breen, November 27 2009.

[xxii] *NewsMax,* "White House Science Czar Involved in Climategate" by L.D. Breen, November 27 2009.

[xxiii] *East Bay Express,* "The New Face of Environmentalism" by Eliza Strickland, November 2, 2005.

[xxiv] http://breitbart.tv/green-jobs-czar-says-white-polluters-steered-poison-into-minority-communities/

[xxv]
http://www.cnn.com/2009/POLITICS/09/06/obama.adviser.resigns/index.html

[xxvi]
http://www.cnn.com/2009/POLITICS/09/06/obama.adviser.resigns/index.html

[xxvii] ABC News, The Blotter, "Air Force One Photo Op Triggers Panic in Manhattan," by Mark Crudele and Lisa Stark, April 27, 2009

[xxviii] ABC News, "New York City Mayor Michael Bloomberg is furious...," courtesy of Dan Matlack and Gustavo Valladares, April 28, 2009

[xxix] *The Daily Caller,* "'Burn a Bush'? Michelle Obama invites rapper Common to a poetry reading," by Neil Munro, May 9, 2011

[xxx] NBCNewYork, "NJ State Police "Outraged" Over Rapper Invite to White House," by Brian Thompson and Marcus Riley, May 12, 2011

xxxi ABC7News Chicago, "240,000 Pack Grant Park for election rally," November 5, 2008.

xxxii *NewsBusters*, Chicago Sun-Times Reports on Deadbeat Democrats, by Mike Bates, February 20, 2009

xxxiii *The Huffington Post*, DNC Finally Reimburses Chicago For Obama's $1.74M Election Night Rally, March 22, 2009

xxxiv *The Hill*, "Obama heckled by protesters at New Hampshire speech," by Bernie Becker and Alicia M. Cohn , November 22, 2011

xxxv *The Daily Caller*, "Red, White and Angry : Communist, Nazi parties endorse 'Occupy' protests," by David Martosko, October 17, 2011

xxxvi *USA Today*, "Occupy protests cost U.S. cities at least $13M," by Associated Press, November 23, 2011

xxxvii *Bloomberg*, "Obama Gets History Lesson From Latin American Leaders," by Helen Murphy and Joshua Goodman, April 18, 2009

xxxviii *The Washington Times*, "Biden to continue collecting rent from Secret Service," by Jim McElhatton, November 10, 2011

xxxix *CNSNews*, "Official Treasury Reports: Coffers Full Enough to Cover Entitlement Programs…," Terrence Jeffrey, July 12, 2011.

xl ABC News, "D'oh! Caterpillar CEO Contradicts President on Whether Stimulus…" by Tahman Bradley, February 12, 2009

xli *Bloomberg*, "Obama Plans To Reduce Budget Deficit To $533 Billion By 2013," by Hans Nichols, February 21, 2009

xliii *National Journal*, "Former Lobbyists Join Obama," by Bara Vaida, January 24, 2011

xliv *Politico*, "Obama finds room for lobbyists" by *Kenneth P. Vogel, Mike Allen,* January 28, 2009

xlv *Politico*, "Obama finds room for lobbyists" by *Kenneth P. Vogel, Mike Allen,* January 28, 2009

xlvi *The Hill*, "Obama: Public is 'sold' on tax increases in a debt-ceiling deal," by Sam Youngman and Alicia M. Cohn

xlvii *The Hill*, "Obama: Public is 'sold' on tax increases in a debt-ceiling deal," by Sam Youngman and Alicia M. Cohn

xlviii *Human Events*, "President Obama is becoming a veritable Pinocchio by stretching the truth on a regular basis…" July 23, 2011

xlix *The Weekly Standard*, "Oops: Obama Breaks Campaign No-Earmarks Pledge in Omnibus Spending Bill,"
By Mary Katharine Ham, February 26, 2009

l *The Weekly Standard*, "Oops: Obama Breaks Campaign No-Earmarks Pledge in Omnibus Spending Bill," by Mary Katharine Ham, February 26, 2009

li *The St. Petersburg Times Politifact.com*, The Obameter, "Go "line by line" over earmarks to make sure money being spent wisely."

lii *Wall Street Journal*, "Obama's Empty Transparency Rhetoric," by Kim Strassel, May 4 2011

liii *Wall Street Journal*, "Obama's Empty Transparency Rhetoric," by Kim Strassel, May 4 2011

liv *The Hill*, "GOP: White House should fess up to lobbyist meetings," by Sara Jerome and Sam Baker – May 3, 2011

lv *The Daily Caller*, "Emails directly link White House to secret transparency meeting," by Jordon Bloom, October 10, 2011

lvi *The Herald-Tribune*, President visits Indianapolis, by Ryan Palencer, May 7, 2011

lvii *The Washington Post*, The Fact Checker, "President Obama's phony accounting on the auto industry bailout," by Glenn Kessler, June 7, 2011

lviii The Heritage Foundation, *The Foundry*, "Morning Bell: Obama's Afghanistan Withdrawal," by Mike Brownfield, June 23, 2011

lix The Heritage Foundation, *The Foundry*, "Morning Bell: Obama's Afghanistan Withdrawal," by Mike Brownfield, June 23, 2011

lx *The Weekly Standard*, "Defining Defense Down," by Gary Schmitt and Tom Donnelly, August 15 2011

lxi FOX ON THE RECORD WITH GRETA VAN SUSTEREN,

November 22, 2011

[lxii] *Wall Street Journal*, "Obama Swing state visits surpass…" by Jonathon Weisman and Carole Lee, November 28 2011

[lxiii] Breitbart TV, "Jake Tapper to Carney: It looks like Obama is campaigning on taxpayers dime" November 28, 2011.

[lxiv] *Los Angeles Times*, "Barack Obama wants to be president of these 57 United States," by Andrew Malcolm, *May 9, 2008*
[lxv] Rushlimbaugh.com, Transcript, Rush Limbaugh, May 12, 2008
[lxvi] Political FactCheck.org, "Obama's Legislative Record," September 25, 2008

[lxvii] FoxNews.com, "White House Move to Collect 'Fishy' Info May Be Illegal, Critics Say," August 07, 2009
[lxviii] *The Blaze*, "Obama Increased National Debt More in 4 Days Than Truman and Eisenhower Did in 10 Years," by Tiffany Gabbay, August 10, 2011
[lxix] http://www.bls.gov/cps/, November 9, 2011

[lxxlxx] www.BLS.gov, Table B-1. Employees on nonfarm payrolls by industry sector and selected industry detail, November 4, 2011
[lxxi] http://www.bls.gov/cps/, November 9, 2011

[lxxii] *The American Spectator*, "The One-Termer We've Been Waiting For" By David Catron on August 4, 2011
[lxxiii] *Associated Press*, "S&P downgrades US credit rating from AAA," by *Martin Crutsinger, August 5, 2011*
[lxxiv] *Bloomberg*, "House Passes $2.1 Trillion U.S. Debt-Limit Increase; Senate to Vote Aug. 2," *by James Rowley and Catherine Dodge,* August 1, 2011
[lxxv] *Bloomberg*, "U.S. Rating Outlook Cut to Negative by Fitch After Deficit Committee Fails," by John Detrixhe, November 29, 2011
[lxxvi] CNN, Erin Burnett Out Front, "Market Rally; Cain's New Accuser; Syracuse Sex Abuse Scandal" aired November 28, 2011
[lxxvii] *The Economist*, "Regulation and the Obama administration, Red tape rising"
January 20, 2011

lxxviii *The Economist*, "Regulation and the Obama administration, Red tape rising"
January 20, 2011

lxxix Rush Limbaugh, "Obama's Lie About Shovel-Ready Stimulus Jobs is Tragic, Not Funny", June 14, 2011

lxxx CNSNews , CBO: Jobs Created and Saved By Stimulus Cost At Minimum An Average of $228,055 Each", by Matt Cover, February 24, 2011

lxxxi *RedState*, CBO Director Admits Stimulus will Shrink Economy'" by Daniel Horowitz, November 15, 2011

lxxxii www.USDebtcolck.org

lxxxiii BigGovernment.com, "Inspector General: Green Jobs Training Program a Failure, Money Should Be Returned" by Publius

lxxxiv *Fox Nation*, "Palin: Fire Holder Now," by Sarah Palin, November 11 2011

lxxxv Townhall.com, "Chris Christie Blasts President Obama: What the Hell Are We Paying You For?" by Daniel Doherty, November 29, 2011

lxxxvi *American Thinker*, "Michelle Blames it on the Kids," **by** Jeannie DeAngelis, **August 27, 2011**

lxxxvii *New York Daily News*, "President Obama's initial reaction to recent terrorist act lacked urgency, decisive leadership" by Daily News Staff, December 30, 2009

lxxxviii The White House Dossier, "E-Day Minus One Year: Golf" by Keith Koffler, November 6, 2011

lxxxix *CNSNews,* "Dept. of Interior: Adding FDR's D-Day Prayer to WWII Memorial Would 'Dilute' Its 'Central Message," by Matt Cover, November 8, 2011

xc *Newsmax*, McCain: Obama's Open Mic Gaffe On Netanyahu Reflects Bad Attitude, by Paul Scicchitano, November 8, 2011

xci *The New York Times*, "Gulf Spill Is the Largest of Its Kind, Scientists Say," by Robertson, Campbell; Krauss, Clifford August 2, 2010.

xcii *ABC News*, "James Carville Slams Obama on Oil Spill Response" by Stephanie Condon, May 26, 2010 [xciii] Political FactCheck.org, "Obama's Legislative Record," September 25, 2008

[xciv] *Washington Examiner*, "With end of Space Shuttle program...," by Rep. Rob Bishop, July 21, 2011

[xcv] *The Hill*, "Perry slams Obama for closing down NASA's space shuttle program," By Alicia M. Cohn, July 21 2011

[xcvi] *The American Spectator*, "Obama Calls Election a "Shellacking," by Philip Klein November 3, 2010

[xcvii] PBS News Hour, "Historic Perspective on Republican Shift," Air date November 4, 2010

[xcviii] *Washington Post,"* Election 2010: Republicans net 60...:" by Chris Cillizza, November 3, 2011

[xcix] Fox News Radio, "Obama Complains about USA to Australian Teens," by Todd Starnes, November 17, 2011